Gerlin Bean

Mother of the Movement

Radical Black Women Series

This series seeks to spotlight the contributions of radical Black women to social justice movements in Britain. It aims to redress, if even in a small way, the dire lack of resources about Black British history in general and Black women's history in particular.

The Black Cultural Archives (London, UK) are publishing partners with Lawrence Wishart for the Radical Black Women Series series.

Forthcoming titles:

Amy Ashwood Garvey and the future of Black feminist archives,
by Nydia Swaby

The Making of June Givanni's Pan-African Cinema Archive,
by Onyeka Igwe

Gerlin Bean

Mother of the Movement

A. S. Francis

Lawrence Wishart
London 2023

Lawrence and Wishart Limited
Central Books Building
Freshwater Road
Chadwell Heath
RM8 1RX

Typesetting: e-type
Cover design: Isabel Lecaros
Printing: Imprint Digital

First published 2023
© A. S. Francis 2023

British Library Cataloguing in Publication Data.
A catalogue record for this book is available from the British Library

ISBN 978-1-913546-37-3
E-format ISBN 978-1-913546-38-0

Dedicated to Gerlin Bean: may her legacy continue to light a path for generations to come.

Contents

Acknowledgements

The following individuals have provided invaluable resources to this project, including their time, consultation, testimonies, source material, and contributions to the recovery process of this history: Zainab Abbas, Hakim Adi, Nzingha Assata, Beverley Bryan, Stella Dadzie, Colin Douglas, Kelly Foster, Neveta Johnson-Fuller, Ama Gueye, Jennifer Hussey, W. Chris Johnson, Brenda Kirsch, Diane Langford, Sue Lemos, Gail Lewis, Deanna Lyncook, Hugh MacCamley, Stephanie Macfarlane, Eric Morier-Genoud, Janet Morris, Lisa Power, Lieda Rosario, Robert Singh, Tony Soares, Olivia Wyatt, Melba Wilson, Ansel Wong, and Jumanah Younis.

Thanks also to the staff at the Black Cultural Archives, Lambeth Archives, London School of Economics Library, National Archives, Senate House, George Padmore Institute, Feminist Library, the British Library, Institute of Race Relations, and anyone I have conversed with about this book, who helped me to articulate and un-muddle my thoughts.

Introduction

*If you were to, say, write a biography of yourself, how would
you wish to be described?*

[laughs] Oh, how would I like to be described?

Or how do you see yourself?

You know, I see myself just as I am, a very committed Black
woman.[1]

Gerlin Bean is most well known for her role in the Black liberation movement in Britain during the 1970s and 1980s. She
was a participant and leading Black feminist theorist in the Black
Power era via the Black Unity and Freedom Party and the Black
Liberation Front, as well as an instigator of the Black women's
movement, wherein she co-founded two of the movement's foremost organisations: the Brixton Black Women's Group (BBWG)
and the Organisation of Women of African and Asian Descent
(OWAAD). Gerlin was born in Hanover, Jamaica in 1939. She
arrived in England as a young woman in 1958 to train as a nurse,
and after some years in healthcare diverged from this career path by
entering into Black revolutionary politics, where she would remain
rooted for over a decade. Although as a post-war Caribbean migrant
she had not anticipated staying in England for more than a few
years, she remained until the 1980s, during that time participating
in – and in some cases founding – multiple Black Power caucuses,
Black women's groups, Gay Liberation organisations, and initiatives to support and uplift working-class youth. Her activism was
not confined to England either; in 1983 she travelled to Zimbabwe
to contribute to post-independence African nation building as an
aid with the Catholic Institute of International Relations, coordi-

nating healthcare and education programmes. After returning to England for a brief time she eventually found her way back to Jamaica in the late 1980s, where she worked tirelessly to advocate and provide tangible support for disabled young people and their families, helping to develop 3D Projects, a pioneering service based in Spanish Town, which exists today as Community Based Rehabilitation Jamaica (CBRJ). With an activist resumé spanning fifty years, Gerlin has made her mark on a multitude of struggles and community networks, always making links between them. Her centrality to the Black radical and Black women's movements of the late twentieth century has not been sufficiently acknowledged by the historical record, much less her other humanitarian efforts.

As we will see throughout this book, these different areas of struggle showcase Gerlin's constant expansion and evolution as an activist, and therefore deserve an increased level of exploration. It is not enough to define Gerlin only as a Black feminist activist or a Black liberationist, although these qualities informed her outlook and practices. Gerlin is an example of an individual who seeks constantly to help marginalised and oppressed members of our global community, and where there are insufficient services for them, to create them and empower people in the process. In viewing these different sites of struggle through the perspective of Gerlin's involvement, we can also reach new levels of understanding about them, their inner workings, prominent ideas and initiatives, and crossovers with other movements. Gerlin's involvement in youth work, for instance, prompts us to consider what some of the major challenges have been for young people, and in particular young Black people, growing up in Britain during the late twentieth century. Her involvement in youth initiatives were interlinked with Black Power politics, and the establishment of supplementary schools, youth clubs, and political education programmes as tools of defence and community control against a racist, capitalist society. At the same time, Gerlin and other politically active women were concerned with the particular issues facing Black women, who are triply oppressed on the grounds of race, class and gender. She constructed Black women's autonomous organising structures from within the Black Power movement, adamant that these two struggles were interrelated and should be treated as such. Then, upon co-founding the BBWG in 1973, she and other women worked on numerous campaigns in collaboration with other activist groups, many of which were male-dominated. Even when faced with misogynist attitudes, Gerlin and other BBWG members remained committed to the tasks at hand, whether it be defending young people against police terrorism in Blacks Against State Harassment (BASH), or as part of the Brixton Defence Campaign in the aftermath of the 1981 Uprisings. When so many intensive years of work in Britain burned her out, Gerlin didn't give up the fight, but instead transferred her energies to a new site of struggle, newly independent Zimbabwe, in 1983. And when she felt it was time to go home to Jamaica, her activism again took on another form, advocating for disabled young people and their families.

The opposite of a self-promoter and a true collectivist, Gerlin's own oral history testimonies – of which there are several – fail to provide us with a full account of her vast contributions. In recent years, the history of contemporary Black activism in Britain and Black women's autonomous organising have gained more attention. But while her important role has received brief acknowledgement, mention of Gerlin in the history books remains condensed to one or two paragraphs at the most. Oftentimes she appears peripherally in relation to other women such as the late Olive Morris, who by contrast has become a well-known and widely celebrated figure in Black British activist history, and whose legacy continues to captivate Black feminists and Black British history enthusiasts. While Olive Morris is often presented as the singular embodiment of a nuanced, collective history of Black women's political organising in Britain, the lack of extensive research on Gerlin (and of course many others) reveals a concerning reality. While organisations such as the BBWG and OWAAD have captured the imagination of contemporary Black feminist activists and writers, they are just one part of Gerlin's story. In the words of Judith Orr, those individuals who worked hard to promote change on the grassroots level 'are rarely named in history books or commemorated in statues or art galleries'.[2] As marginalised histories grow in popularity and edge closer to the mainstream, so too are many people written *out* of history. Historical accounts are repackaged and distorted. Complicated movements and events are condensed into repetitive narrations, credited to a handful of individuals. All in all, the state of the historical memory of Gerlin Bean is in dire need of recovery. In the last several years, however, as writings relating to the history of Britain's contemporary Black movements have increased, the frequency with which we can locate Gerlin's name in written works has also improved. Natalie Thomlinson, Tanisha C. Ford and W. Chris Johnson are among the short list of writers who have made a point of emphasising Gerlin's role as a leading member of London's Black Power network, founder of many key Black women's organisations throughout the early to mid 1970s, and subsequent recruiter and mentor for other activist women.[3] In addition to these works, since beginning the writing of this book, a Wikipedia page about Gerlin has been constructed, a long overdue yet greatly encouraging development. The historical record as it stands most commonly refers to Gerlin via her leading work in the Black women's movement in Britain during the 1970s and 1980s, and her affiliation to the BBWG and OWAAD. Although a notable portion of her history, these organisations are just two pieces in the enormous puzzle that we will seek to assemble in this book. It's also important to state here that, alongside the important research conducted by the writers listed above, the loudest calls for recognition for Gerlin have come from the community of activists in which she belonged, including but certainly not limited to voices such as Zainab Abbas, Nzingha Assata, Beverley Bryan, Stella Dadzie and Gail Lewis.

I first met Gerlin Bean in June 2018, in the café of the Black Cultural Archives in Brixton. Our meeting came after a year and a half of my trying to get in contact with her. She was accompanied by her friend Denise, who I found out during the course of the day was a former member of the Black Panther Movement. I had not long finished my undergraduate dissertation, entitled 'No Liberation Without Black Women: Gender in the Black Liberation Front'. This research had provided a window into Gerlin's work in the Black Power movement, and had been greatly aided by the guidance of Zainab Abbas, who first introduced me to Gerlin's story and told me of the great disservice that the historical record had done to her, describing her as 'the most underrated woman in the movement'.[4] In the time between this revelation and my meeting with Gerlin I conducted some research, and was shocked, but not surprised, that someone who had been so heavily involved in the Black radical movement of the late twentieth century, and was crucial to so many key organisations and political campaigns, could have been so overlooked by historians, researchers, and those who claimed to be interested in Black feminist history. It had not been easy to get in contact with Gerlin and organise a meeting, and I hoped it would be the first of a series, to attempt to recover as much of her story as possible. During the meeting, it was clear that Gerlin was all too aware of her omission from history and was interested in the prospect of it being recovered. I'd prepared some interview questions to get the ball rolling, but not long into our conversation she laid out the ground rules for our encounter: this was to be a session where she would recount some of her memories of her time in the struggle and I would listen, and once she was reassured of my intentions we could organise follow up sessions. Over the course of the day, Gerlin and Denise recounted some of their fondest memories of the Black Power era, as well as the challenges – of which there were many. This interaction also gave me a taste of Gerlin's great sense of humour, humility, and revolutionary optimism. It was hard not to be in awe, hearing stories I had read about from her in person, and listening to a woman who had pioneered fearlessness, interconnectedness across struggles, leadership and unwavering commitment to social change. Although this was not the last time I met Gerlin, the future interview sessions we discussed never came to fruition. Gerlin's health began to seriously decline, and she was eventually diagnosed with Alzheimer's disease.

In light of these events, this book has taken on a different shape than I had initially envisioned. My original aim was to conduct a series of interviews with Gerlin, mapping out different chapters of her life from childhood to the present, and using her own words as the driving force of the story, with some contextual aids. This method was not envisaged arbitrarily, but rather due to the importance for Black women, where possible, to document our own histories, and control our own narratives. As Heidi Safia Mirza voiced within her project of assembling Black British feminist theorisations, 'In writing about our world, our place on the margin, black feminists take the risk of what happens when we expose ourselves as objects of study. Laid bare by our unveiling, our inner-most life stories become objects for public gaze; our resistance is known. We engage in naming our subjectivity, telling our story'.[5] This is no longer possible for Gerlin, and highlights the sheer urgency of such recovery projects. As each day passes, we are losing more and more vital recollections from people to whom we owe so much, and who owe it to ourselves to learn from. This book's research is therefore made up of a tapestry of accounts from Gerlin's prior interviews, as well as testimonies from of Gerlin's family, friends and comrades.

In the first chapter we aim to piece together the sparse information on Gerlin's early life in Jamaica and consider the historical context of her upbringing, to understand how her experiences growing up informed her outlook on the world and her position within it. This brings us to her migration to England as an eighteen-year-old student nurse who was recruited into the NHS. Within this second chapter we view England through her eyes as a new arrival: her encounters with British racism, cold weather and labour relations, as well as grappling with motherhood and her burgeoning concern for the issues facing Britain's Black communities in the 1950s and 1960s. The third chapter traverses Gerlin's activities that were specifically geared towards protecting, uplifting and mentoring young people, and in particular young Black people located in London's inner-city areas, during the tumultuous decades of the 1970s and 1980s. From here, we move into a study of Gerlin's participation in revolutionary politics in the fourth chapter, from Black Power to the women and gay liberation movements. It is here that we can better appreciate the myriad of struggles she was connected to, her vast understanding and capacity as a revolutionary theorist, and her ability to develop her knowledge and impart it in the projects and networks which she helped to build. The fifth chapter is dedicated to highlighting Gerlin's role as a leading architect of Britain's Black women's movement and Black socialist feminism, and this chapter also provides a deeper exploration into the organisations she helped to nurture, their structures, challenges and political evolutions. This takes us to the last stage of her political biography when, in the early 1980s, she departed England and expanded her activity to cover new areas such as helping with nation-building efforts in Zimbabwe and developing a lifeline for children with learning difficulties and their families back in her home country of Jamaica. It seemed to me, when drawing all of these aspects of Gerlin's life into one text, that there was no more fitting way to end than with a selection of testimonies from those who worked alongside her. Thus, the final section of this book, Chapter Seven, contains short reflections on Gerlin's impact and legacy written by her friends and comrades.

This book represents the great collective effort that goes into salvaging underrepresented histories. Without the willingness, generosity, and support of Gerlin's people, this work would have been an impossible feat. Due to the integral presence of these testimonies, the story has become not only a biographical charter of Gerlin's own political journey, but also that of her contemporaries. This book seeks not only to rescue and celebrate Gerlin's story but that of a particular generation of Black radical activists, and a particular era in history which feels simultaneously close and far away. Another important pillar of this book's research has been the collection of archival sources, those which have found their way into the safety of public archives, and those which have been carefully stored in people's private collections. This book's fundamental aim, then, is to present Gerlin's legacy as wholly as possible, by placing it within a wider context. But this research project was not only prompted by the lack of existent work on Gerlin at the time of writing; it was also inspired by an awareness of the potential that Gerlin's story has for inspiring younger generations to study the methods of her and her comrades in tackling the conditions caused by racism, imperialism, patriarchy and capitalism. Hopefully, once this historical picture becomes a more complete one, younger generations will stand in better stead to continue these struggles. This book is, primarily, an attempt to recover as much of Gerlin's journey as a political activist as possible. I do not claim to have recovered all of it – it is very much an ongoing process. This book represents the beginning of the task, and I hope to be joined by many others in this effort.

NOTES

1 Gerlin Bean, 'The Heart of the Race: Oral Histories of the Black Women's Movement', Black Cultural Archives: ORAL/1/3, 2009, p40.

2 Judith Orr, *Marxism and Women's Liberation,* Bookmarks: London, 2015, p23.

3 See Chapter 5 of Tanisha C. Ford, *Liberated Threads: Black women, style, and the global politics of soul,* The University of North Carolina Press: Chapel Hill, 2015; Natalie Thomlinson, *Race, Ethnicity and the Women's Movement in England, 1968-1993,* Palgrave Macmillan: London, 2016. See also W. Chris Johnson, '"The Spirit of Bandung" in 1970s Britain: The Black Liberation Front's revolutionary transnationalism', in Hakim Adi (ed), *Black British History: New Perspectives from Roman Times to the Present Day,* ZED Books: London, 2019.

4 Zainab Abbas, personal comment to the author, 17 March 2018.

5 Heidi Safia Mirza, *Black British Feminism: A Reader,* Routledge: London, 1997, p19.

Early life

I always wanted to come back home because my basic foundation was here, and so I don't care how hard it is here that's
where I know.[1]

Gerlin Adassa Bean was born in Hanover, northwest Jamaica,
on 10 February 1939, the third eldest of seven children.[2]
According to her birth certificate she was born in the district of
Mount Hannah, in George's Plain Mountain. Her father was Ralph
Bean and his occupation was recorded on the birth certificate
simply as 'labourer', although the family also owned their own land.
Her mother was Melgata Bean, née Spence.[3] At the time of writing
not much is known or recorded about her early life other than basic
details and anecdotal snippets. Despite the small amount of information, what we do know helps to provide an indication of some of
the early influences on Gerlin that helped to shape her worldview,
and the settings that nurtured her in her youth. Gerlin was born at
the tail end of a significant epoch in the rich history of movements
for liberation and self-determination in the Caribbean. The West
Indian labour rebellions, as they are known, swept across the region
between the years of 1934-1939. Jamaica, as the most populous
British Island in the Caribbean, was particularly inflamed with
workers' uprisings. The Great Depression, which lasted from 1929-
1939, had seriously impacted the colonial economies of the
Caribbean islands, which were already organised in favour of white-
owned plantations and corporations at the expense of the largely
African Caribbean labour force. However, the global economic

downturn, poor working conditions, increasing unemployment levels and a steep decrease in quality of life created a situation ripe for a widespread and prolonged militant response from the masses. It is difficult to discern how much Gerlin's own family were affected by the economic conditions of the time given the minimal descriptions she provided on the occasions she was interviewed in adulthood. But suffice to say she was born during an intense moment of political activity, one in which the struggle for workers' rights and national independence from colonial rule was heightened, and she would later contribute to these same struggles as they reignited throughout the latter part of the twentieth century. The Jamaican Communist activist, Trevor Carter, described the impact on this period of anti-colonial unrest on him and Gerlin's generation thus: 'Those of us who came to Britain in the fifties had grown up in a period of sustained political activity at home ... This movement touched everyone's lives and a strong sense of solidarity bound us together in the face of an easily identifiable enemy, British imperialism'.[4] In this chapter, the available information on Gerlin's early life has been pulled together and placed within this historical context. The main aspects of her upbringing that we are interested in here are her journey through the education system and any political influences that might have impacted her as she grew into her activism in adulthood.

Gerlin grew up in a rural neighbourhood and her parents worked as farmers, a typical profession in Hanover at the time. She went to school in Westmoreland Parish, just south of Hanover, first attending Grange Hill Primary School and continuing to secondary education at Manning's School in the neighbouring parish of Savannah la-Mar, Westmoreland. These facts relating to her schooling are important to examine alongside the context of the times, and the system of education under colonial rule more generally. Prior to the nineteenth century, formal education was scarce in the British Caribbean. The schools that did exist were privately funded and existed to educate the children of the wealthy planter class, and later a small number of schools for the poor were established using bequests from wealthy individuals.[5] Manning's is the oldest continuously operating high school in Jamaica. Its history, like so many institutions in the Caribbean, is intimately connected with the legacy of slavery. It was founded in 1738 initially as a free school for poor white children. The land and funds used for the school were bequeathed by Thomas Manning, a slave owner based in Burnt Savannah, Westmoreland. In recent years, there have been calls to rename the school due to this history – a campaign Gerlin would no doubt have supported.[6] Prior to Jamaica's independence from British colonial rule in 1961, the education system was heavily modelled on Britain's educational system and its maintenance of class structures. The curriculum served as imperial propaganda. Members of Gerlin's generation often remark that they therefore knew more about Britain than those living in Britain at the time, and learned little to nothing about their own surroundings in the Caribbean, or the rest of the world for that matter.[7] The colonial education system performed an important role in espousing the apparent superiority of 'Great Britain', conjuring a positive image of the British Empire and fostering subservience among the people of the Caribbean. Similarly to the rest of Britain's empire, the education system in the Caribbean performed a key function in maintaining the colonial order. Its educational policy aimed to prepare the colonised population to take up the roles designed for them in the labour market. This meant allowing a degree of social upward mobility for the middle classes and providing only a rudimentary education for those expected to take up agricultural or industrial work.[8]

Alongside this economic function, education also worked to decimate the cultural heritage of Caribbean people, the majority of whom are African descendants, and to this end it is viewed as one of the 'most damaging tools of imperialism, because it has inculcated populations from a young age with ways of understanding themselves as culturally worthless'.[9] Amílcar Cabral's speech 'National Liberation and Culture' remains one of the most insightful articulations on the need for dominating forces to suppress a people's culture in order to maintain systems of oppression: 'Culture is simultaneously the fruit of a people's history and a determinant of history, by the positive or negative influence which it exerts on the evolution of relationships between man [sic] and his environment, among men or groups of men within a society, as well as among different societies'.[10] What impact this might have had on

Gerlin, and her responses to the education she received, is worth thinking about. As we will see in later chapters, in adulthood she was actively involved in curating alternative spaces of education that instilled cultural pride, confidence and revolutionary curiosity in young Black people. In any case, education was an indispensable gateway to obtaining a better quality of life, and of course better job and economic prospects. Thus, despite its shortfalls, it was highly valued by Caribbean peoples, and Gerlin understood this well. During an interview in 2009 Gerlin reflected on the importance of obtaining an education in Jamaica, and indeed the consequences of its nonattainment, in the context of attempting to mobilise people in Jamaica to examine how society and the state are structured, and how to organise against its oppressive nature:

> It's got to do with a consciousness, which is dependent on the level of literacy, education. So one of my things is about – it doesn't matter if it's the 'white man's education', or whoever's education, if you can get some education – and it hasn't got to be university level, just to be able to read and understand it. And that's why I'm sorry for lots of poor children, especially in Jamaica, the young children I don't want to fail, especially the boys, who are not understanding, and then you can't reason at that level of understanding. One of the old Jamaicans who came up and could hardly read, he couldn't understand when his daughter is trying to understand the police and [how] they're part of this arm of the state that comes to oppress you, so if you don't understand, how [can] we try to break it down?[11]

This perspective was widely shared, and was especially pertinent for Black women growing up in the colonies, as the authors of *Heart of the Race* addressed: 'Education has always been a burning issue for Black women. Viewed, in the aftermath of slavery, as virtually the only means for us and our children to escape the burden of poverty and exploitation, it was regarded in the Caribbean as a kind of liberation. Our families made enormous sacrifices to send us to school, even though they could often offer us only the most basic education'.[12] In accordance with this, the fact that Gerlin remained in school right up until the age of eighteen is also interesting. Prior to independence, receiving both primary and secondary education in the Caribbean was not a given, and as Gerlin attested to above there are still major challenges related to accessible and equal education, as class dichotomies persist. Even as late as 1960, around 15 to 20 per cent of primary school-aged children didn't attend school due to lack of access.[13] In comparison to other territories of the British Empire, the British Caribbean had more primary schools, but the number of children actually in school fluctuated and could be as low as 50 per cent in some areas. Despite the existence of a compulsory education ordinance, because there were not enough primary schools available it couldn't be enforced.[14] Thus, the onus lay on children's families to prioritise education in spite of the obstacles. Regarding secondary education, the situation was even more difficult. Depending on the financial situation within a family, a child might be expected to leave school at primary age or drop out of secondary school before completion in order to find work. This was more common for girls than boys. Some took up jobs to help support their families, others left to help care for their younger siblings, and others had to leave or attend very infrequently if their family couldn't afford the expenses that came with attending school.[15] The fact that Gerlin received a full education indicates that her family were financially stable and upwardly mobile enough to permit her to attend, and that their attitude toward education was positive. Gerlin hinted at their support of her educational journey when she recounted the process of being recruited as a student nurse by the British government at the age of eighteen: 'My parents were very worried that I would waste my time here, have babies, and the rest would be history. So they were really glad for this programme and off I went'.[16] Clearly they were aware of the gendered barriers that existed for women in Jamaica, and saw a career in nursing as a way of securing a positive future for their daughter.

Outside of school life, historian W. Chris Johnson has suggested that her childhood surroundings put her in good stead for future political organising in Britain, commenting that 'she was nurtured by traditions of communal living and mutual aid'.[17] During an interview with Johnson, Gerlin recalled that there was a strong

'African tradition' in the local community, and that Marcus Garvey and Garveyite ideas were discussed by the adults, although her age prohibited her from understanding their significance.[18] Garveyism, a Black nationalist movement that advocated Black entrepreneurism, Pan-Africanism and celebration of Black history and culture, was hugely influential in the early to mid twentieth century, especially in the United States and the Caribbean, so it is of little surprise that Garveyism would have been a prevalent topic of discussion among Gerlin's community. Jamaican creative, performer and scholar Honor Ford-Smith summarised Garveyism as 'unquestionably, the most influential anticolonial organisation in Jamaica prior to 1938'.[19] However, by 1937 Marcus Garvey had lost credibility in the eyes of workers, radical activists and even members of the Universal Negro Improvement Association (UNIA), the organisation which he founded and used to propagate his philosophy far and wide. This downturn was particularly strong during the West Indian Labour Rebellions, due to his conservatism and refusal to blame colonialism for the ills faced by the Caribbean working class.[20] Despite his wavering popularity, the movement he created remained significant in promoting the importance of education and self-reliance for people of African descent. It is also noteworthy because women were highly active in the movement, and were encouraged to be politicised and educated. These principles of the Garvey movement were in no small part due to the influence of Garvey's wives, Amy Ashwood and Amy Jacques Garvey.[21] The endurance of Garveyism is attested to in Gerlin's recollection of her experience of the movement as a child. Although the politics which she developed throughout her adulthood were different to Garveyism, being based more on socialism, on her return to Jamaica as a seasoned activist Gerlin helped to organise Marcus Garvey commemorations and was active in promoting the ideas and legacy of Garvey in the nation of his birth (see Chapter Six).[22]

In adulthood, Gerlin was the only one of her siblings to involve herself in activism of any kind, and her other siblings have been described as more traditional.[23] And so, although her upbringing might have provided a good reference for community-oriented ideas and an appreciation of her African heritage, Gerlin's path in life was perhaps more greatly influenced, as we will see throughout this book, by her own inclination as an individual, her passion for societal liberation and transformation, and the journey she charted to involve herself in such projects. There is, however, the possibility that more information around Gerlin's upbringing and family might surface in the future and challenge this assumption. In addition to the educational and political context of Gerlin's early life, there are almost no available recollections on Gerlin's general family life, but what is available is worth discussing. On one occasion, during an interview in 1971, Gerlin described her childhood as content, and mentioned that her parents seemed to have a good relationship with each other, although there was some level of disagreement between them due to her mother's disciplinarian style of parenting. This was as much detail as Gerlin thought necessary to give. Gerlin's recollections of her early life, when she has divulged them, are not personal or anecdotal but extrospective. As we can see from the below description of her parents' relationship, during interviews she sought ways of tying in her personal story with analyses of norms and developments of the Black family unit, and wider societal constructs:

> I suppose [my parents] have quite an ordinary relationship. They had their little rows, but it was quite good. My father and mother seemed fairly happy together. We were happy as kids. My mother was fairly dominant; she would beat the kids, slap them or something, whereas my father has never really touched us. They used to have rows about that. In the black family the mother seemed to dominate the kids.[24]

Aside from this brief remark about her parents, and thanks to the research efforts of Gerlin's daughter Jennifer, we now know that Gerlin's father Ralph spent time working in the United States before later settling in England, following a common migratory pattern for Caribbean people in this period. It could be assumed that his travelling for work contributed to Gerlin's view of her mother as the dominant parent, as well as her specific parenting style.[25] In oral history, interviews and conversations of the kind that Gerlin participated in several times throughout her life can reveal much about the subject's personality, their personal development over their lifetime, and how they construct their life experiences into a narrative.[26] One might refer to a specific memory to address a question, one might provide very concise answers so to not give too much away, and one might also skilfully pivot around an interviewers' questions, angling a conversation toward certain topics only that they wish to talk about. Gerlin's own style as an interviewee exemplifies her humbleness, humour, light-heartedness – but also an unwillingness to discuss her personal life in much detail. With the exception of her 1971 *Shrew* interview, it's clear that in other interviews such as the 'Heart of the Race: Oral Histories of the Black Women's Movement' and the 'Do You Remember Olive Morris? Oral History Project', she didn't regard her early life as relevant to the topic of discussion, and so did not divulge much about it. The interviewer for the 'Heart of the Race' project asked her to start from the 'beginning', which in this context meant the beginning of her involvement in the Black women's movement:

If you could maybe start at the beginning

[laughs] Do you really think I remember the beginning?

Well as much as you can remember from the beginning about how you kind of got involved in the movement.

Ok, erm was it 1970? It's sometime in the 1970s. There was a conference in Oxford.[27]

Then, later on, the interviewer attempted to ask Gerlin about her early life growing up in Jamaica, and whether she recalled any events that might have influenced her in later life. Gerlin responded in a way that left this question unanswered, and returned to her life in Britain:

So, growing up, are there any particular experiences that kind of –

Oh, me growing up?

Drove you, yeah, drove you into –

Well look I grew up here... In Jamaica. I went to England when I was eighteen so I'd grown up and I –

Whereabouts here?

In Hanover... I was born in Hanover, went to school in Westmoreland

Ok

So I have two parishes, and then I went there and it was surprising. I went there to be trained as a nurse because the Tory government, they came here I was at Manning's, I was just young, and they came here recruiting nurses.[28]

Although the interview included discussion of what Gerlin was working on in Jamaica at the time of the interview in 2009, neither Gerlin nor the interviewer prompted a discussion of Gerlin's early life again. In this oral history series, the interviews were conducted by a number of interviewers, and so there is some variation in the questions asked and how they were framed, although the overall focus remained the Black women's movement. Sometimes the interviewers prompted a discussion into the interviewees' childhood, such as the below example of an interview with Linda Bellos, conducted by a different interviewer. This had the desired effect of producing a reflection on early life influences, organically opening up the interview into a biography:

Can you spell your Nigerian name, repeat it and spell it, please.

Bandile – B-A-N-D-I-L-E. Adebowale A-D-E-B-O-W-A-L-E. My father was Yoruba he was born in a place called Uzeba, near Lagos. He came to England – he was born in 1917 – he came to England during the war in 1942.

Does your Yoruba name have a particular meaning in English?

It does. I think it's something like 'come home'. I think my name is 'come home', my first name.

But when you were growing up, you were called Linda?

I mean my English name is Linda, but my Nigerian name, I mean for family events you know, I'm Bandile – I was when I was a child.

OK. Well actually that is something I will want us to talk about a little bit, about you growing up, but before we actually delve into the interview, I wanted to ask you, given that we do have limited time, if there were any particular historical events that impacted you.

Sharpeville.

Sharpeville? OK.

As a young child. I was born in 1950 and I think that I, I think that I was quite politically aware. Um, what I do know about the year I was born is that there were 30,000 black people/people of African origin in the United Kingdom, um when I was born which is a very small number and I suspect that within spitting distance of this place, there are more than 30,000 black people so, it kind of gives you an idea of how small our community was, um, and it would be fair to say that the majority population made me very conscious that I was a black child.[29]

Of course, the fluid nature of conversation and memory can take an interview in any number of directions, which means that oral history often opens up more questions in the process of providing some answers. The outcome of interviews are determined by both the interviewer and the interviewee's personality, conversation style and aims for the process, as well as the overall brief of the oral history project that the interviewer is responding to, and the dynamic between the two people. I recognise from my own experience of meeting Gerlin for the first time – arriving at what I thought was an interview, but what turned out to be a friendly vetting process – that she is cautious about who she recounts her story to and how much of it she recounts. Gerlin didn't seem to be more open about her early life with her friends and comrades in Britain either. Zainab Abbas, one of Gerlin's oldest friends, doesn't recall Gerlin ever speaking about her early life or family at a substantial length.[30] The strict focus on the period of the Black women's movement in her two oral history interviews paired with her considered evasion of this period of her life in conversation help to explain the dearth of material on Gerlin's childhood. It seems fair to say that she left this chapter of her life behind her when she departed for Britain.

NOTES

1 Gerlin Bean, 'The Heart of the Race: Oral Histories of the Black Women's Movement', Black Cultural Archives: ORAL/1/3, 2009, p46; hereafter BCA.

2 Jennifer Hussey in conversation with the author, 11 April 2023.

3 Birth certificate provided by Jennifer Hussey.

4 Trevor Carter, *Shattering Illusions: West Indians in British Politics*, Lawrence & Wishart: London, 1986, p18.

5 Anne Spry Rush, *Bonds of Empire: West Indians and Britishness from Victoria to Decolonization*, Oxford University Press: Oxford and New York, 2011, pp22-23.

6 Dr Rovan Locke, 'As we treat Cecil Rhodes, so must we treat Thomas Manning', https://wiredja.com/index.php/op-ed/as-we-treat-cecil-rhodes-so-must-we-treat-thomas-manning, 7 June 2021.

7 Rush, op cit, p21.

8 Saran Stewart, 'Schooling and Coloniality: Conditions Underlying "Extra Lessons" in Jamaica', *Postcolonial Directions in Education*, Vol 4, No 1, 2015.

9 Mark V. Campbell, 'Indigenous Knowledge in Jamaica: A Tool of Ideology in a Neo-Colonial Context', in *Anti-Colonialism and Education: The Politics of Resistance*, Sense Publishers, 2006, p195. Of course, there is also a sizeable population of people of Indian descent in the Caribbean due to the history of indenture. For more on this see Gaiutra Bahadur, *Coolie Woman: An Odyssey of Indenture*, Hurst & Company: London, 2013.

10 Amílcar Cabral, 'National Liberation and Culture', Eduardo Mondlane Memorial Lecture Series, New York, 20 February 1970.

11 Gerlin Bean, 'Do You Remember Olive Morris? Oral History Project', Lambeth Archives Department: IV/279, p19.

12 Beverley Bryan, Stella Dadzie and Suzanne Scafe, *Heart of the Race: Black Women's Lives in Britain*, Virago, 1985, p59.

13 Rush, op cit, p24.
14 Arthur Lewis, *Labour in the West Indies: The Birth of a Workers' Movement*, New Beacon Books: London, 1977.
15 Hermione McKenzie, 'The Educational Experiences of Caribbean Women', in *Social and Economic Studies*, Vol 35, No 3, 1986, p68.
16 Gerlin Bean, 'No, We Didn't Burn Our Bras', in Hilary Robertson-Hickling (ed), *That Time in Foreign*, Hansib, 2016.
17 W. Chris Johnson, '"The Spirit of Bandung" in 1970s Britain: the Black Liberation Front's revolutionary transnationalism', in Hakim Adi (ed), *Black British History: New Perspectives from Roman Times to the Present Day*, Zed Books: London, 2019, p129.
18 W. Chris Johnson, email exchange with the author, 5 December 2022.
19 Honor Ford-Smith, 'Unruly Virtues of the Spectacular: Performing Engendered Nationalisms in the UNIA in Jamaica', *Interventions*, Vol 6, No 1, 2004.
20 Christian Høgsbjerg, '"A Thorn in the Side of Great Britain": C. L. R. James and the Caribbean Labour Rebellions of the 1930s', *Small Axe: A Caribbean Journal of Criticism*, Vol 15, No 2, 2011, pp38-39.
21 For more on this, see Nzingha Assata, *Women in the Garvey Movement*, York Publishing Services, 2008.
22 W. Chris Johnson, email exchange with the author, 5 December 2022.
23 Jennifer Hussey in conversation with the author, 11 April 2023.
24 Gerlin Bean interviewed in *Shrew*, September 1971, p11.
25 Jennifer Hussey, correspondence with the author, 13 July 2023.
26 Trevor Lummis, *Listening to History: The authenticity of oral evidence*, Barnes and Noble Books: Totowa and New Jersey, 1988, p21.
27 Bean 2009, op cit, pp1-2.
28 Ibid, pp10-11.
29 Linda Bellos, 'The Heart of the Race: Oral Histories of the Black Women's Movement', BCA: ORAL/1/4, pp1-3.
30 Zainab Abbas in conversation with the author, 27 June 2023.

2

Migration to Britain and nursing career

I was shocked. It was shock, because I didn't know anything about racism at that time.[1]

In 1958, at the age of 18, Gerlin was recruited onto a student nursing programme for the NHS. It was this event which led to her migration to England. She travelled by plane, and was collected by her brother who was an RAF pilot and already settled in England. Not long after arrival she was given a job in Bethnal Green General Hospital in the East End of London.[2] Because of her enrolment on a nursing programme, Gerlin was able to avoid two immediate problems that faced many other newly arrived Black migrants: employment and accommodation. She had already secured employment, and with this came board in the student nurses' home (the cost of which was deducted from student nurses' monthly pay packet). The third problem facing Black people – that of British racism – was not so easily evaded. It was during her time as a student nurse that Gerlin had her first encounters with this form of discrimination, as we will see. The circumstances of Gerlin's migration to Britain from Jamaica is by now a familiar story from that era; she was a part of a collective journey that many African, Asian and Caribbean women took in the post-war period, as members of the Commonwealth, to what was then the 'motherland', or the imperial core.[3] Her nursing career only spanned around eight years. So far, biographical accounts of Gerlin do not focus much on her work as a nurse. Rather, the oral history interviews conducted with Gerlin focus on her activism in the Black movement broadly, and the Black women's movement more specifically.[4] Gerlin herself has also tended not to elaborate on her nursing years past a brief mention, presenting this part of her life as a precursor to the activities she was more passionate about. The richest source on Gerlin's nursing days comes from a lecture she gave as part of a series organised by Hilary Robertson-Hickling entitled *That Time in Foreign*.[5] There are also several appearances of Gerlin on records such as the British electoral register and nursing register, which provide some semblance of a timeframe for her nursing. In any case, this period of her life was an important chapter that provided her with insight into post-war British society, its pervading racism and labour relations. It also acted as a stepping-stone into other caring professions such as community work, to which she later became deeply committed. This section is therefore dedicated to understanding the circumstances of Gerlin's migration, how and why she initially sought a nursing career, her immediate reactions to life in England, her experiences of racism in nursing and her response to it.

Alongside many other women, Gerlin was recruited into the NHS in the post-war period during a labour shortage. As early as 1949, the Ministries of Health and Labour, the Colonial Office, General Nursing Council and Royal College of Nursing worked together on a policy of recruitment from Britain's colonies in general, and the Caribbean in particular.[6] The historical narrative of Black women's role in the NHS is often framed as helpful colonial populations responding to calls to succour the understaffed health service, ignoring the important role of race, class and colonialism in their decision to migrate. The NHS was one of numerous fractured industries in post-war Britain; other such industries included London Transport, which similarly recruited people from the Caribbean to mitigate labour shortages. This phenomenon is treated in much the same way as the contributions of African, Asian and Caribbean peoples in the Second World War, who 'came to the aid' of Britain in a time of crisis. However, from an anti-colonial standpoint it is obvious that both these instances were products of the dynamic between colonial powers and subjugated colonial, or former colonial, communities – a systemic exploitation of resources, including human labour. As Beverley Bryan has pointed out, the depiction of the post-war generation of Black people who settled in Britain as 'good negroes who came, worked hard and were treated badly' is not only problematic and uncritical but inaccurate.[7] Long before the creation of the NHS, working-class Caribbean people were used to moving to wherever there were decent job prospects. These moves were often motivated by high rates of poverty and unemployment in their countries of origin, general underdevelopment caused by colonialism, and the devastation left behind by hurricanes and tropical storms (this was especially true of Hurricane Charlie in 1951). Popular destinations included other islands, Britain or the United States. However, after 1952 the US was no longer a viable option, as the McCarren-Walter Act severely restricted entry to the US in a deliberate effort to halt Caribbean migration. There were thus several push factors which influenced the post-war wave of migration to Britain.[8] In the words of *Heart of the Race* authors, 'England was seen as the Promised Land simply because prospects in the Caribbean were so limited'.[9] Between the late 1940s and mid 1950s the number of people entering Britain from the Caribbean increased each year. But by the late 1950s these numbers declined. In 1958 around 30,000 people arrived from various Caribbean nations, Gerlin among them. That number then dissipated in 1962, due in large part to the British government's racist Commonwealth Immigration Act, which according to the Communist and Black radical activist Claudia Jones, 'established a second-class citizenship status for West Indians and other Afro-Asian peoples in Britain'.[10] Despite these barriers, the NHS continued its recruitment of overseas staff. Between 1966 and 1967, there were 16,745 trainee nurses and midwives from overseas, 75 per cent of whom were of Caribbean origin.[11]

From available research on the recruitment of Caribbean women in the decades after the NHS was founded, it's evident that many were motivated to join by their aspiration for a better future for themselves and their families, utilising new environments and job opportunities as a means to forge their own destinies and leave behind stagnant national economies and limited prospects. This chimes with Gerlin's own reasons for pursuing a career in nursing. In the Caribbean nursing, alongside teaching, was a highly regarded job role. As a caring profession, it was well-respected and offered a certain amount of social status. Nursing had traditionally been a profession for middle-class women, and prior to the creation of the NHS it was not a career path open to working class women in England, much less working-class Black women from overseas. Although the prestigious image of nursing might have inspired young women to take up recruitment advertisements, Gerlin herself has not indicated that she possessed any affinity for it, implying that the decision for her to enrol in the student nursing programme lay with her parents and their aspirations for how her life might be.[12] Gerlin signed up when the recruitment campaign reached her secondary school, Manning's. The school would have been a fitting location to host a recruitment event. To qualify, prospective students had to be literate, possess GCSE-equivalent Maths and English qualifications, and in Gerlin's words, have 'a little bit of intelligence'.[13] The required age-range was between 18 and 30.[14] As a recent Manning's graduate, Gerlin qualified.

Beyond the recruitment stage, the experiences of Black staff in the NHS during the 1950s and 1960s has revealed common threads of racial discrimination, from workplace bullying and confining Black staff to the least pleasant tasks and shifts to blocking career progression. Although many women such as Gerlin were recruited into nursing positions, Black women were employed predominantly in the lowest paid roles such as domestic cleaners and canteen workers, and those in nursing were filtered into geriatric and psychiatric nursing, which were viewed as the least desirable areas of nursing. Black doctors, similarly, were overrepresented in psychiatry and geriatrics.[15] Black women have since reported on their experiences as student nurses in various history projects, and their testimonies include many similarities.[16] For example, one woman recalled that during her SRN training her and other Black as well as Irish staff were repeatedly given the worst job of cleaning bed pans in the sluice. Her testimony also reveals a sense of powerlessness that student nurses felt at the time:

> I arrived in England in 1951, to pursue a course in nursing at a hospital in London. During my career as a student nurse, I came across a series of problems with nursing sisters who make you go to the sluice all day to wash waste from incon-

tinent patients. It was very difficult then to figure out why it was always the few Black nurses and Irish who got sent down to the sluice ... There were other aspects of nursing duties to be done, but invariably you end up in the wretched sluice, either cleaning bed pans or washing the messy bed sheets. Freezing cold, freezing but you had to accept it, though you knew it was wrong.[17]

Up until the 1980s there were two avenues for prospective nurses in Britain: State Enrolled Nurse (SEN) and State Registered Nurse (SRN). The SEN qualification took two years of training to obtain, whereas the SRN took three. There was a significant disparity between the long-term prospects that each of the two avenues provided. Generally, the SEN qualification required less educational qualifications and severely limited the likelihood of career progression. The SRN qualification usually required more educational qualifications by comparison and provided a direct track toward the position of Ward Sister. In addition, SEN qualifications were not recognised outside of the UK so for those who planned to train in Britain, qualify and return to their homelands, it was of no use. But the distinctions between the two nursing qualifications were not always explained to Black women, and many were actively encouraged to train as SENs, or refused entry onto SRN programmes.[18] Given that Gerlin enrolled onto an SRN programme, she may have possessed high qualifications from school, and/or was aware of the need to obtain the SRN qualification if she wished to utilise it back in Jamaica. Looking back on her time as a nurse, Gerlin noted that her experience was likely better than that of many other Black women. In the one instance where she relayed a more in-depth account of her nursing days, she tied it in with an analysis on the general situation of Black women employed in healthcare:

Lucky for me, my experience wasn't that bad – but if you read the history of some nurses, it's really, really bad. They've been abused and used, underpaid, they were told they'd come to be a State Registered Nurse (SRN) or a Registered Mental Nurse, and they end up being what is called a State Enrolled

Nurse (SEN). Many of these persons were well qualified from back home. They were teachers, from different professions, looking for better lives or some more money – because they were told there was better. Therefore, that's what they did, they gave up everything and they came, and then that's what happened.[19]

Although it has now been confirmed that Gerlin arrived in England in 1958 and began her training in that same year, these details were at first difficult to pinpoint because the information varies from source to source. And while so much of Gerlin's story has been captured by oral history projects, which have proven invaluable to researching this book, her testimonies from these projects don't always provide a coherent timeline. For example, during her interview with *Shrew* magazine in 1971 Gerlin stated that she 'came over here in 1960 to do my nursing and then to go back,' so in the past it has been claimed that 1960 was her year of arrival.[20] But in an interview in 2009 with the Black Cultural Archives she said, 'I went to England when I was 18, that was 1958, 1959 … so now you know how old I am, I was 18'.[21] Gail Lewis, a leading figure in the Black women's movement and one of Gerlin's close friends and mentees, also confirmed in an interview that Gerlin had arrived sometime in the late 1950s.[22] When searching for mention of her name in nursing and electoral registers, I couldn't find anything prior to 1962 – which indicated that she didn't complete her training before this year. Upon learning that she conducted her training at Bethnal Green General Hospital, I gained more clarity and direction on where to look next. After gradual cuts to its services over the 1970s and 1980s, Bethnal Green Hospital ceased to operate in the early 1990s, and surviving records were deposited at Barts Hospital Trust's archive. Thanks to the help of the archivists there, we can now be sure that Gerlin was in England from at least October of 1958. Admittedly, what does exist in Bethnal Green's records pertaining to Gerlin is limited. Although the hospital's files include a sizeable collection of photographs of nurses in the years Gerlin was present, she is not featured in any of them. Interestingly, although Gerlin is absent from the photographs, they demonstrate that the hospital recruited a large number of Black nurses from the 1950s onwards, many of whom would likely have been recruited in similar circumstances as Gerlin.[23] Whether the cohorts of Black nurses there developed support systems for each other was not mentioned by Gerlin but seems likely given the circumstances they were faced with in Britain at this time, even if these support systems were predominantly social. Alongside her anecdotes on the time she spent at the hospital, this gives us at least some idea of her activities as a student nurse, and the important role that this placement played in exposing Gerlin to British racism. It also suggests that this may have impacted her relationship with the nursing profession and begun to steer her in other directions. Gerlin's first impressions of life in England were based on her immediate surroundings in the East End, and the wintery weather: 'I went in one of the batches and went straight to a hospital down in the East End and stayed there for a while. I really didn't really like it. 'Cause it was so cold, I can remember, it was so dark. At that time they used to have the fog'.[24] In the hospital's Preliminary Training School Register, Gerlin appears as 'G. A Bean'.[25] This register details nothing more than the courses that student nurses attended and the length each course ran to. Such brief information is useful at least for providing a timeline of Gerlin's presence at the nursing school. It also gives us some insight into the topics on the student nursing curriculum at the time.

According to this register, Gerlin attended the school from 1 October 1958 - 1 January 1959. She undertook classes in Anatomy and Physiology, First Aid, Theory of Nursing, Bacteriology, Beds, Practical Settings, Cookery, Personal and Communal Health, Bandaging, Psychology, Visits, Films, Demonstrations, Nutrition, and Hospital Details. Alongside this, Gerlin also conducted practical training on three wards in the hospital. It was during her time on the wards that Gerlin encountered racist attitudes from patients: 'What turned me off very quickly was what I was told by patients … So here I was, one of my tasks was to bathe this old lady and I went with my water and everything well prepared as a good nice nurse. I said, "Good morning ma'am, I've come to give you your bath." She starts screaming and she says, "Get away from me!! Get this black thing out of here! Take your black hands off me!"'[26] This kind of verbal abuse from patients was all too

common for Black nurses. But it was not something that they were
trained to expect or would necessarily have encountered before,
given their recent arrival from the Caribbean, and often they were
not supported in how to deal with it. For Gerlin, this interaction
served as a wakeup call to the inherent existence of racism in the
healthcare service, constructed within a society shaped by racism,
imperialism, class and capitalism. As one former NHS worker
remarked, it reminded her 'very much of a colony in the way it's
run ... the white sister will act as manager, organising the work for
her Black nursing staff, and then spend the morning sitting in the
office'.[27] Suddenly, the strange sense she had been picking up on
from other staff members began to make sense: 'Before that I used
to get a little funny feeling from people, from staff, and I just said
well we're culturally different ... So it didn't bother me'.[28] Gerlin
now understood it was indicative of the larger issue of racism,
which was prevalent in the NHS just as it was in British society
in general: 'I was shocked. It was shock, because I didn't know
anything about racism at that time. I was eighteen. I was from the
country. The most I've ever seen [of a white person] would have
been a missionary, so I didn't know about all this. In the church
everyone is nice and polite, so I wouldn't have experienced that. So
now I thought, wow, is that what it was about?'[29]

It's important to note that in the same year as Gerlin's arrival to
Britain, violent, coordinated, racist riots swept the areas of St Ann's
in Nottingham, and Notting Hill in London. Although Gerlin was
not yet living in England when these riots broke out, she came to
know about them later on, and acknowledged their significance
in the long, historic struggle against racism in Britain. She drew
particular inspiration from the responses of Black women during
the riots, who were at the forefront of community resistance: 'I
wasn't around at that time, but I was told that women were there
side by side fighting physically, against those white racists'.[30] Black
women were also at the forefront of anti-racist organising strategies
and campaigning in the aftermath of the riots, including Claudia
Jones, Amy Ashwood Garvey and Frances Ezzrecco, to name a few.
Taking place over the summer of 1958, the racist riots in Notting
Hill were particularly intense, lasting several weeks. On one night,
a mob of around 2,000 racist young people descended on the

Notting Hill area, where it was estimated that between 3,000 and 5,000 Caribbean people lived at the time, mostly in poor quality housing.[31] This was the atmosphere in which Gerlin and thousands of others arrived. Racism and anti-immigration sentiments were rife, and racial discrimination was not illegal in Britain until the passing of the Race Relations Bill in 1965. This act was met with much criticism from the anti-racist movement, as it only covered incitement of racial hatred in public areas, and left institutionally racist practices in housing, employment and other realms of society untouched. After its passing, many workers felt it had little to no effect on reducing racist incidents. Prior to the Bill, the frequent racial discrimination that Black and Asian people experienced in Britain during the early to mid twentieth century was referred to as the 'Colour Bar'. It was a widespread practice used by employers, landlords, pubs and institutions. They could refuse entry to people on the basis of their perceived race without legal repercussions. In many instances the police helped establishments to enforce the colour bar by escorting Black people from establishments where they had been turned away.[32]

Britain's hospitals, similar to many other service-providers, practised the colour bar by largely refusing to hire Black people as medical staff. During the 1930s, Black women wishing to become nurses were barred from doing so (with some notable exceptions). This led the Jamaican activist, poet and broadcaster Una Marson, along with the League of Coloured People (LCP), to launch a campaign to enable Black women to be admitted to train as nurses in British hospitals. Upon protesting the Manchester Royal Infirmary's decision to deny a Black woman's application to train as a nurse in 1937, the hospital wrote back to the LCP that: 'We have never taken coloured nurses for training here. The question was a definite rule that nobody of negroid extraction can be considered'.[33] Although the creation of the NHS later led to the necessity of including Black people in hospital employment strategies, the structural racism which had brought about the discriminatory practice in the first place remained deeply rooted. Black nurses, just like other Black workers in Britain, couldn't rely on their workplaces or trade unions to support their struggles. It was not until the 1980s that trade unions responded to the demands of Black and Asian workers and began efforts to include their concerns over racism in trade union agendas. Not only this, there are various examples of racial discrimination from the unions themselves in the first several decades of the NHS's existence, and in some cases unions launched campaigns to oppose the recruitment of 'coloured' staff in Britain's hospitals. Black nurses therefore had to rely on their own initiatives and communities to find ways to deal with racism at work. Reactions from Black nurses varied; some attempted to ignore instances of racism and push through the daily tasks at hand, others found it more difficult to shrug off, or fought back in small ways.[34]

Speaking at 'That Time in Foreign' lecture series at the University of the West Indies in the 2000s, with years of experience behind her, Gerlin looked back on her encounters with racism during her nursing days with a wider analysis on the function of racism in the NHS: 'Racism is a fundamental thing in all these places. It's so embedded in the conscious of the people that they're saying it without realising it …' Of the specific instance of racist verbal abuse from an elderly patient, Gerlin relayed how this revelation of British racism inspired an attempted escape out of the nursing profession:

When [it] came out like that then I thought – yes, this is where my nursing stops. Nobody is going to cuss me. But guess what? I didn't realise that we were contracted, so you just couldn't walk … I was a little rebel from long time. I wrote to my sister in Jamaica. I said, send me a telegram quickly. Say my mother is very ill and I have to come back home … This telegram came and I went to the matron and said, 'Matron, I have to go back to Jamaica, my mother is really ill.' I wasn't going back to any Jamaica … She said okay and she released me and asked when I was coming back. I got into trouble later on though, here was this matron following me up. She had written home to my parents who knew nothing about it … So I had to come clean and explain. They were cool, so I stayed on.[35]

After this event Gerlin moved out of the nurse's home and stayed with a friend for a while, where she enjoyed more freedom to socialise and explore. Life in a student nurse's home was restrictive, as student nurses were under the supervision of a home sister. It was during this time away that Gerlin began a relationship with a man, fell pregnant and gave birth to her daughter, Jennifer. Throughout the pregnancy she envisioned that she would marry Jennifer's father, but she wanted to wait until after the child was born in case 'he'd think it was a ploy'.[36] 'By the time I had her', Gerlin explained, 'I didn't want to get married'.[37] Finding herself a single mother, and with her nursing training incomplete, Gerlin decided to transfer from general to psychiatric nursing, moving to Warlingham Park Hospital, a psychiatric facility in Surrey. Nursing as a profession carried with it certain lifestyle expectations: it was frowned upon to be married or to have children. Gerlin arranged to have Jennifer privately fostered at six months old; she was subsequently placed with a local elderly English couple. Although Gerlin moved back to London several years later, Jennifer didn't move in with her until the age of thirteen. She spent some time living with an aunt before moving in with her mother full time. Gerlin explained her rationale for the decision in 1971: 'I wouldn't move her [Jennifer] because it would be upsetting, until I take her eventually to stay'.[38] Private fostering, also sometimes referred to as 'farming', is a private, informal arrangement made for children below the age of sixteen to be placed in the care of someone who is not a relative, for a period of more than twenty-eight days. It was a common practice during the 1950s and 1960s among West African parents who came to England primarily to study. They wanted their children to have a stable routine and access to British cultures and values, as they believed such access would provide the children with a better chance to excel in British society.[39]

It was slightly less common for Caribbean parents to have their children privately fostered in this way. Many parents who migrated from the Caribbean in the post-war period left their children with family in their home countries, sending for them later. These children became known as 'barrel children'. Because Jennifer was born after Gerlin's migration this option was not possible, and we might assume that Gerlin had limited childcare options available to her that would allow her to continue nursing. As the most discerning analysis of the general conditions for Black women in Britain in the twentieth century, *Heart of the Race* provides an important reminder that 'in the early 1960s, the State was still busy trying to encourage (white) women to stay here and embrace domestication and consumerism. It wasn't prepared to offer any childcare support to Black women who had to work. In such a climate, we were compelled to develop other strategies'.[40] Both the private fostering system and the barrel children phenomenon had consequences for children in the long-term. Those who signed up for the role of private foster parents were usually working-class white women, who were 'well-intentioned, if misdirected – they just wanted a child without the hassle'.[41] Usually private foster parents lived in the home counties of Kent, Surrey, and East Sussex. Many people who experienced the private fostering system have since detailed the trauma associated with being separated from their own culture, issues with identity, fractured bonds with their biological parents and in some cases neglect and abuse at the hands of their foster parents. This was of course not everyone's experience, but the high number of children who were harmed by this system was increasingly reported on by the media, healthcare professionals and concerned parents. In Jennifer's case, she recalls that her foster parents 'did their best as older English people', but she was the only Black child in the schools that she attended. When the time came to move back in with family, Jennifer experienced a culture shock, 'through moving from English to traditional Caribbean and then from traditional to unorthodox and highly politicised Black Power households'.[42]

From 1961 onwards Gerlin was working at Warlingham Park Hospital as a student psychiatric nurse, and was listed on the electoral register with the hospital as her residential address.[43] She qualified on 11 December 1963, and thus appeared on the 1964 nursing register. It seems that Gerlin found her time at Warlingham Park better than her previous placement; she seemed to suggest her personality was perhaps better suited to this type of hospital: 'I went back into nursing but I did psychiatric nursing then, and that was much better. It was quite fun for me because all of us in there seemed a little bit mad ... everybody seemed a little bit touched, so it didn't really matter, so we had great fun in that situation'.[44] After this stint living and working just outside of London, Gerlin returned again to general nursing in Lambeth Hospital. During this time she completed part one of midwifery training: 'I did Part One Midwifery and then I gave up. It was a good foundation. I am not disappointed that I had that training'.[45] This qualified her to deliver babies in hospital, however midwives required both part one and two of their training in order to qualify as District Midwives and therefore respond to call-outs in the local area.[46] She appeared again on the nursing register in 1966.[47] This is the end of her appearances on nursing records, which indicates that she left the profession sometime during that year. Gerlin turned her attention toward community work and grassroots political organising and, as we will see, the experiences she procured during her nursing days proved invaluable reference points. In 1966, by the time Gerlin hung up her nursing hat once and for all, she had become well-versed in the entrenched nature of British racism, as well as the connections between racism, colonialism and labour exploitation. In the years to come she leaned on her direct experiences of nursing in theorising the specific oppressions faced by Black women in Britain, and Black nurses as a significant group within the Black British community.

NOTES

1 Gerlin Bean, 'No, we didn't burn our bras', in Hilary Robertson-Hickling (ed), *That Time in Foreign*, Hansib: London, 2016, p149.

2 Ibid, p148.

3 The historical presence of Black women in Britain's healthcare sector has been explored in a number of projects, including: Young Historians Project, 'A Hidden History: African women and the British Healthcare Service, 1930-2000', www.younghistoriansproject.org/research-hub, 2021; BBC, 'Black Nurses: The Women Who Saved the NHS', www.bbc.co.uk/programmes/b083dgtb, 2016; Lynn Eaton, 'The story of black nurses in the UK didn't start with Windrush', www.theguardian.com, 13 May 2020; Ann Kramer, *Many Rivers to Cross: Caribbean People in the NHS 1948-1969*, Stationery Office: London, 2006.

4 I am referring to 'Heart of the Race: Oral Histories of the Black Women's Movement', held at the Black Cultural Archives (BCA), and 'Do You Remember Olive Morris? Oral History Project', held at Lambeth Archives Department, both conducted in 2009.

5	This lecture series culminated in the book by Hilary Robertson-Hickling, *That Time in Foreign,* Hansib: London, 2016.

6	Kramer, op cit, p16.

7	Beverley Bryan, 'A Brief History of Key Moments and Issues in the Black British Civil Rights Movement', *BlackInk,* Issue 2, September 2021, p1.

8	See Peter Fryer, *Staying Power: The History of Black People in Britain,* Pluto Press: London, 1984, pp378-382; David Olusoga, *Black and British: A Forgotten History,* Pan Macmillan; London, 2016, pp491-500.

9	Beverley Bryan, Stella Dadzie and Suzanne Scafe, *Heart of the Race: Black Women's Lives in Britain,* Virago: London, 1985, p22.

10	Claudia Jones, 'The Caribbean Community in Britain', *Freedomways,* 1964.

11	Kramer, op cit, p20.

12	Robertson-Hickling (ed), op cit, p148.

13	Ibid.

14	Kramer, op cit, pp16-18.

15	Diana Watt and Adele D. Jones, *Catching Hell and Doing Well: Black Women in the UK – The Abasindi Cooperative,* UCL Institute of Education Press: London, 2015, p21.

16	See the Young Historians Project, op cit; BBC, op cit; Bryan, Dadzie and Scafe, op cit, pp17-57.

17	Unnamed speaker, 'Roots Oral History Project' (1992), referenced in Watt and Jones, op cit, p22.

18	Ron Ramdin, *The Making of the Black Working Class in Britain,* Verso, 1987, pp311-312.

19	Bean 2016, op cit, p150.

20	Gerlin Bean interviewed in *Shrew,* September 1971, p10.

21	Gerlin Bean, 'The Heart of the Race: Oral Histories of the Black Women's Movement', BCA: ORAL/1/3, 2009, p12. In all of her interviews, Gerlin refers to her age at the time of her arrival in the UK as eighteen. It is possible that she was in fact nineteen, if she arrived after her birthday in February 1958. However, since no documentation of the date of her arrival has been located so far, I have followed her suggestion that she was eighteen at the time she came to the UK.

22	Gail Lewis, 'The Heart of the Race: Oral Histories of the Black Women's Movement', BCA: ORAL/1/21, 2009, p8.

23	Photographs from the Bethnal Green Hospital collection, Barts Hospital Trust archives: RLHBG/P.

24	Bean 2009, op cit, p12.

25	Register of student nurses for the Preliminary Training School, January 1958 - January 1963, Barts Hospital Trust archives: RLHBG/N/2/5.

26 Bean 2016, op cit, p148.

27 Bryan, Dadzie and Scafe, op cit, p45.

28 Bean 2016, op cit, p149.

29 Ibid, p148.

30 Gerlin Bean in a letter to Stella Dadzie from Harare, Zimbabwe, 27 July 1984. From Stella Dadzie's private collection.

31 The Institute of Race Relations, '"Coloured people in Great Britain": Summary of press news and comment, September 1958', 16 October 1958, pp4-5.

32 For an example of the colour bar and significant protests to it by working-class Black activists such as Len Johnson, see Shirin Hirsch and Geoff Brown, 'Breaking the Colour Bar: Len Johnson, Manchester and anti-racism', in *Race & Class,* Vol 64, No 3, 2023, pp36-58.

33 The League of Coloured Peoples, 'The Manchester Hospital and Coloured Nurses', *The Keys,* Vol 4, No 3, 1937.

34 For examples see Bryan, Dadzie and Scafe, op cit, Chapter One.

35 Bean 2016, op cit, p149.

36 Bean 1971, op cit, p11.

37 Ibid.

38 Ibid.

39 For more information on the private fostering of West African children in Britain see Jordanna Bailkin, 'The Postcolonial Family? West African Children, Private Fostering, and the British State', in *The Journal of Modern History,* Vol 81, No 1, 2009, pp87-121.

40 Bryan, Dadzie and Scafe, op cit, p29.

41 Fundación Emmanuel, *Spreading the Wings of Foster Care,* 2003, p403.

42 Jennifer Hussey, correspondence with the author, 6 May 2022.

43 Register of Electors, 'County of Surrey', 1962.

44 Bean 2016, op cit, pp149-150.

45 Ibid, p150.

46 Tania Staras, 'A Brief History of District Midwifery', *AIMS Journal,* Vol 34, No 3, 2022, p14.

47 General Nursing Register 1966, p6.

3

All our future is in our young people – youth initiatives

All our future is in our young people ... I feel that we need to be able to give up. When I say give up – hand over, right? Train up so we can hand over to the young people so you have the thing going on.[1]

By the mid 1960s racism was firmly planted in all aspects of society in Britain, and hostile reactions to the increased presence of Black and Asian people after the Second World War made settling in Britain a task of survival and defence. Housing, employment, health, education, immigration policies and policing were some of the main areas where racism and discrimination were most apparent. Many young people had witnessed the struggles of their parents, who had migrated to the UK in the 1950s and early 1960s, and understood from an early age that they could not depend on the state to protect them. With each discriminatory law that was passed in parliament, it became increasingly obvious to young people that it was the British State who stoked the fires of racism. The Commonwealth Immigrants Act of 1962 was updated in 1968 by a Labour government eager to satiate hostile sentiments toward racialised people in the aftermath of Enoch Powell's infamous 'Rivers of Blood' speech, in which he declared: 'Nothing will suffice but that the total inflow for settlement should be reduced at once to negligible proportions'.[2] The government remained anxious to find new ways of restricting the entry of Black and Asian peoples in Britain and suppressing the rights of those already present. Historian Peter Fryar described how, 'between 1958 and 1968, Black settlers in Britain watched the racist tail wag the parliamentary dog'.[3] As the decade of the 1960s drew to a close this was still the case, as evidenced by the 1971 Immigration Act. The Act targeted New Commonwealth citizens not of 'British stock', and still forms the basis of today's immigration policy, creating the conditions for the Windrush scandal.[4] For people who were already settled in the UK, the demand was that they assimilate to Britain's cultures and norms and make as little noise as possible.[5] Young Black people who were either born in Britain or migrated during childhood to join their parents became recognised as 'second generation immigrants', and bore the brunt of racism in the education system as well as on the street. One manifestation of racism which directly affected young people was the disproportionate rates by which Black children were labelled educationally subnormal (ESN), an outcome of the pseudoscientific notion that Black people were intellectually inferior to their white counterparts. These ideas were publicly professed by educational institutions such as the Department of Education and Science (DES), who in a 1965 Circular endorsed the myth that Black students were intellectually inferior and posed a 'problem' to the school system. The Circular recommended local authorities adopt a policy of 'dispersal' to ensure 'immigrant' children didn't make up more than 30 per cent of a given school's population.[6] This was then incorporated by the Labour government in a White Paper. In addition, Section 4 of the 1824 Vagrancy Act experienced a renaissance, as police wielded the power to stop, search and arrest anyone they thought *might* commit a crime, without the need for evidence.[7] This became known as the SUS law, and translated into unrelenting harassment and brutality, especially for young Black people residing in Britain's inner cities. Seeing what young Black people were dealing with inspired Gerlin's move into community work:

> I started out as a Nurse and I thought, well you seek and you get better, but there was so much happening to our Black youths, because the SUS law at that time was very prevalent, and you could be looking at a car, 'oh that's nice', and the alarm goes off and the police would arrest you on suspicion to

break in, so we had lots of youths who were being criminalised. And I thought, we need to work with our young people
... I thought all our future is in our young people, and lots
of our Black men – young men – and women – were being
brutalised and criminalised. So, if we could prevent that
somehow, which you can't in a sense, because in a racist environment there will always be that ...[8]

After her move away from nursing, Gerlin worked on a number
of initiatives specifically designed to provide support, enrichment
and safety to Black working-class youth across London, who were
becoming a terrorised and increasingly oppressed section of society.
Gerlin did not work in isolation, but operated within a growing
network of concerned activists. Prominent figures included Jessica
and Eric Huntley, John La Rose, Gus John, Ansel Wong and many
others. The late 1960s and early 1970s saw the development of a
supplementary school movement, particularly in the aftermath of
Bernard Coard's influential 1971 publication, *How the West Indian
Child is Made Educationally Subnormal in the British School System.*
This publication vindicated Black communities, confirming their
suspicions that the problems facing Black children in education
were neither the fault of the children themselves nor their parents,
but were caused by the institutional racism of the school system.
As Coard argued, Black children's identities were being 'destroyed'
in mainstream schooling, as they were constantly 'belittled' and
'ignored'.[9] Coard linked the dire situation of Black children in
British schooling with the wider operation of British imperialist
capitalism, arguing that the school system worked to prepare 'our
children for the society's future unskilled and ill-paid jobs', just as
their parents' generation had been actively recruited for 'unskilled'
and 'dirty' jobs in the post-war years.[10] From at least 1966 if not
before, Black parents and community members began developing
support schemes for young people. Their aims were not only to
provide supplementary education but also to assist working parents
with childcare, and to ensure young people were not left unsu-
pervised on the street where they would be vulnerable to police
harassment. As a result, community-run supplementary schools,
youth clubs and play schemes sprouted up across Britain.[11] Gerlin

knew that while the system which allowed racist state violence to flourish remained intact, there was a limit to what she could do on the ground to mitigate the oppressive conditions experienced by Black youth. But as we will see, her growing awareness of how the white supremacist capitalist system operated only spurred her on in the fight to build an alternative, and uplift young people in the process. This chapter will present Gerlin's activities that had a specific youth focus, and illustrate the dynamic methods she deployed as a youth worker from the late 1960s into the 1970s.

SEVENTIES COFFEE BAR

Gerlin's first entry into youth work was at the Seventies Coffee Bar, a youth club in Paddington. Set up by Westminster Council, the idea for a coffee bar as a space for young people had first been articulated by local Labour Councillor, Illtyd Harrington, in 1961. During a speech at the council meeting, Councillor Harrington claimed that the Tory councillors viewed the Paddington borough as one 'large Butlin's camp'. He urged councillors to help prevent the growing 'gangsterism' of the local youth and pointed to various issues such as alcoholism and poor sexual health, as well as a recent event wherein two local boys went out on a rampage to beat up 'coloured' people. His proposal was that the council put £5,000 towards developing a coffee bar for young people.[12] Given that nothing was done for several years, we can assume his plea fell on deaf ears and the problems continued. By 1967 Councillor Harrington renewed his plea for a council-owned coffee bar/youth club scheme. The *Marylebone Mercury* reported of his plans for an upcoming meeting: 'He will urge the council to consider making a shop available in the Harrow Road for use as a coffee bar by young people where "suitable control" can be exercised'.[13] His suggestion was this time taken on board by the council, and in September 1968 it was announced that the project would go ahead. The *Mercury* reported: 'The Council of Social Service is planning to convert the premises at 470 Harrow Road. There will be a basement discotheque for dancing, a ground floor coffee and snack bar, with office and living accommodation on the upper floors'.[14] But there was again

some level of hostility to this plan, and a week later the *Mercury*
reported that some citizens were calling for the coffee bar scheme
to be completely scrapped. The President of the local Ratepayers'
Association complained that 'the whole principle is wrong. There is
far too much money being devoted to young people who ought to
be looking after themselves'. After some delays the Coffee Bar eventually opened in 1970. Sometime before its opening, Gerlin applied
to the job post advertised by Westminster Council and began work
on the scheme. Prior to opening she worked on designing the
services that the Coffee Bar would provide.

As a staunch anti-capitalist who was informed by the Marxist-
Leninist principle of liberating all sections of the working-class,
Gerlin understood that it was not only Black youth who were nega-
tively affected by the economic and political system but indeed
all youth. In the first year or so, The Seventies Coffee Bar was
frequented mainly by white young people due to the demographics
of the area. It was an eye-opener for Gerlin to some of the specific
issues that the local youth were facing, from high instances of drug
use to poor school performance. It was obvious to Gerlin that
although they were not dealing with the additional component of
racism, they were experiencing significant challenges that required
creative approaches to solve them:

> The interesting thing about this one was that when I got the
> job it was to work with white working-class youths. That's why
> I did a coffee bar, so that they could drop in, we physically
> fixed up the basement so that they could have a recreational
> space – and they were on glue. They were all sniffing glue as
> they truanted from school, they were all over the place sniffing
> away there. Getting a high. A few of them used to smoke pot,
> but it was mostly the glue they got hooked on. Here I am
> this black woman now to run this project for all these white
> youths. Can you believe it? So because I was in charge of this,
> I employed two white males and two white females. We had a
> staff of five for the Coffee Bar. We worked with them. We did
> a lot of things, counselling, games, everything. We got them
> back into the education system.[15]

Then, as Gerlin observed, the demographics of the local area began to shift, leading to encounters with young Black youth in the coffee bar. This again required a shift in tactics, as these young people were now dealing with the various forms of racism mentioned above:

> What happened was that poor black youths moved in. Now this was a different ballgame, because they were also into a lot of different things. They had more than the white youths, because then we had the police harassment to go with it.[16]

In light of this added complication to the lives of the young people there, Gerlin began attempts to build a rapport with the police station on the Harrow Road. She hoped that in doing so, they'd be less inclined to harass the young people associated with the Coffee Bar, but this was unsuccessful. The Coffee Bar was subjected to frequent police raids, where police looked for any evidence of drug possession or other criminal activity to charge the young people with. The young people soon put a system in place to avoid being caught out, which included having a look-out stationed outside the Coffee Bar, who'd alert those inside when the police were on their way in. Then, any young people in possession of anything illegal had time to flush it down the toilet. Gerlin and the other staff were aware of this system. As she explained, by not coming down hard on the young people for activities such as this, she and the other staff were able to develop better relationships with the young people:

> People may think that is negative and you're condoning that kind of behaviour – but when you get into the psyche of the kids, the young people you're working with, then you can relate to them in a different way. You can build a relationship, because they know you understand where they're coming from and then you can get through to them ... So with that methodology we were getting them back onto a correct track for their own self-esteem and self-development.[17]

It was this empathetic, laid-back approach that Gerlin would take with her into all youth work, and which became her signature style of leadership. As we've explored so far, the issues faced by the young people of the Seventies Coffee Bar were linked to issues outside of their home lives. However, Gerlin also had to navigate the complicated dynamics between young people and their parents, and the misunderstandings between generations. As more Caribbean children appeared at the Coffee Bar, Gerlin observed the cultural divide between the young people who were being socialised according to their British environment and their parents, who held traditional Caribbean values. There were, of course, gendered dimensions to these issues too, which Gerlin also had to negotiate. For example, she found there were crises developing between parents and their teenage daughters that had various root causes, from fractured relationships caused by years of separation due to the barrel baby system, religious and cultural differences between the two generations, anxieties surrounding girls' sexual activity, and poor housing conditions, which caused or exacerbated tensions between family members. In response to these issues, Gerlin evolved into both a youth worker and family counsellor. She established a girls' group as part of the Coffee Bar's programmes, having identified that the girls required a space to discuss topics specific to their experiences. Gail Lewis, who had met Gerlin and was taken under her wing, was invited to some of the group's sessions, as a local. Gail recalled the significance of such a group in what was at the time a predominantly white area, with limited nearby resources for those interested in Black politics and culture:

> I was living at home, my mum and dad were living in the Harrow area between Willesden and Kenton at my maternal grandmother's house. And then it was a very white area. Albeit very working class, white working class … so you didn't really have access to radical black literature and stuff like that. It was inevitable that you had to travel in. So I did that. And then Gerlin made contact with me and we exchanged numbers, phone numbers and stuff like that. And she invited me a couple of times to the girls group that she was running in the Harrow Road. [She] was running this in the youth centre, [it] was really radical to be running a girl's group with a political bent, under the cover of Local Authority financing if you see

what I mean, service financing. And it was very much my first introduction to an idea that girls and women, but girls really, needed some kind of support of their own to develop their own agency.[18]

It seems that, as the 1970s was such an intensive period of activity for Gerlin, in later life she neglected to mention this aspect of her work at the Seventies Coffee Bar in interviews. She did, however, report on it in her 1971 *Shrew* interview, when this work was ongoing:

> I am doing work with adolescent girls at the moment and quite a bit of case work with families and their daughters. They are mostly West Indian families. They seem to be having more difficulties with their daughters. They are very religious – Catholics – and they don't want their daughters to go out. They keep locking them up. These girls, when they get about fifteen, want boyfriends and other friends – they want to go out in the evening – so the least chance they get they run away from home. I try to find them. I see the girl and I talk to her and try to explain the difference between living in England and living in the West Indies, and the generation gap between a fifteen-year-old and her mother. I try to relate to them in that way and take them home and explain the same thing to the parents. The parents have got their own difficulties and I sit and listen to them. It's nice to have someone just listening … it's not just the daughter running off – it's the flat they're living in which is in very poor condition; or they are living in a very cramped situation … it's the generation that's growing up now, that came here between the ages of six and eleven. That in itself is a trauma: leaving school, coming to a different place and their whole system is upset. Another significant thing is when the parents come here before the child. The child then comes out and is a total stranger to the parents. And the parents cannot understand this. I also play a supportive role to some of the girls who have young babies and haven't got support from anyone else. All sorts of things like finding jobs and finding accommodation because it is all part of it.[19]

There is one significant event from Gerlin's Seventies Coffee Bar days that she viewed as symbolic of her growing role as a respected community figure and a protector for young people besieged by racist policing. During an altercation between police and regulars of the Coffee Bar, three young people were arrested and taken to Harrow Road police station, causing a stir among the local community. Soon the road was filled with concerned parents, friends and neighbours demanding their release. Due to the central role that the Coffee Bar played in the event, Gerlin assumed the position of spokesperson for the crowd, as well as advocate for the young people under arrest:

> I was there and I had to support [the young people] whether I wanted to or not ... They would not let anyone else speak to them, I was the one who had to speak. Here I was a buffer between them and the police and I'm saying ... 'let them out, otherwise Harrow Road is going to burn'. It's true, it would happen, because people had had enough. The police conceded in a very sheepish way.[20]

Gerlin was required to stand surety for the young people and ensure they attended court. After signing their bail, they were released. The protest by the local community was a success in that it achieved its aim of securing release for the three people, and Gerlin played an important role in this as mediator. Nothing more came of the standoff; after the young people's release the crowd dispersed, with Gerlin ensuring everyone departed safely:

> They were really disciplined youths. They didn't mash up anything, they just stood firm. The youths came out, they went home, I hung around and made sure everybody went home because they all came from the community and there were no further incidents.[21]

Although no confirmed press coverage of this event has been recovered, there is reference to an event that bears some similarities in two issues of the *Marylebone Mercury* between November and December of 1972. This newspaper focused on the court proceedings and made no reference to the notable community turnout that Gerlin recalls taking place. Instead, the first article entitled 'Court story of punch up outside youth club' harnesses police testimony to describe an initial clash between police and young people outside the Coffee Bar on 16 July 1972. The opening line positions the police as vulnerable and the young people as confrontational: 'A woman police officer was trapped by an angry group of about 70 coloured youths when they clashed with police outside a Paddington youth club'.[22] The article suggests that the crowd of young people were initially waiting for the Coffee Bar to open, and that when police officers appeared to question two girls about an assault on a white girl, they encircled the officers and began 'punching and kicking' one of them. The article then goes on to list the details of three young men who were arrested and subsequently charged with assault and threatening behaviour, and a fourth who was arrested sometime later, also for threatening behaviour. They all denied their charges.[23] The second article, 'Youth put boot in – Magistrate', provides some more insight into the nature of the altercation, referencing testimony from one of the defendants: 'during the course of the hearing allegations were made about the police "bullying" a nine-years-old coloured boy. [The defendant] claimed that he went to help the boy and had to hit at the officer in self-defence'.[24] If this is related to the same event, which prompted a large community response and thrust Gerlin into a position of leadership, the precise details are less important. What is significant is that the experience of running the Coffee Bar was Gerlin's first exposure to a role of community advocate, and provided her with the tools and experience needed to further take up the mission of shielding young people, and young Black people in particular, from institutional violence. Whilst Gerlin was doing important work in Paddington, she was not yet collaborating with other Black community workers. In addition, the Coffee Bar was a product of Westminster Council, and although it provided a safe space and supportive services for local young people, it was not connected to Black liberation politics, and had no radical elements to its programme. It was her next job role which put her on the map as an influential figure in London's world of Black community work, and which many people associate her with.

GRESHAM PROJECT

In 1973 Gerlin left the Seventies Coffee Bar in Paddington to assist
with setting up the Gresham Project in Brixton. The origins of the
Gresham Project can be found in the historical struggle of Black
parents who were campaigning for welfare initiatives to nurture their
children's educational and cultural identities, and protect them from
state racism. In 1968 the Caribbean Education and Community
Workers' Association (CECWA) was established. A large part of its
remit was to investigate the treatment of Caribbean children in the
British school system, who were being disproportionately labelled as
'Educationally Subnormal' and generally miseducated. A conference
was organised by the CECWA where Bernard Coard, then working
as a teacher in East London, presented his research findings, which
were eventually published as *How the West Indian Child is made
Educationally Sub-normal in the British School System*. The late
Gloria Cameron, a parent and member of CECWA, invited Coard
to Brixton, where other local parents were already discussing what
should be done to support Black children. This set the ball rolling,
and regular parents' meetings were held to come up with viable solu-
tions. One outcome of this was the Gresham Project, run by the
Council for Community Relations in Lambeth.[25] The Project had
a physical home on Gresham Road opposite Brixton Police Station,
a contentious setting given the violence experienced by the local
community at the hands of the police there. The Gresham Project
operated as a youth club, general support network and supplementary education centre, and was connected to Ahfiwe Supplementary
School. The late Reverend Tony Ottey, a well-known and respected
figure in the local area, who like Gerlin hailed from Westmoreland,
Jamaica, was brought on as the Project's manager.[26] He was joined
by Gerlin, who worked as the Project's full-time community worker,
and Ansel Wong, who worked as the Principal of Ahfiwe. Ansel was
also a teacher at Sydenham Girls School, an activist with the West
Indian Students Centre, and a key member of the Black Liberation
Front (BLF), a pan-African, socialist and Black Power-oriented
group based in northwest London.

As part of a nationwide initiative by Black parents, community
workers and activists, the Gresham Project represented a specific

approach to cultivating learning opportunities and educational development outside of the confines of classroom structures. This movement in Britain drew on a much longer praxis of community-driven education, such as the prevalence of supplementary lessons, or 'extra lessons', as they were commonly referred to in the Caribbean, where children would receive teaching outside of the classroom on evenings or weekends to supplement limited or inaccessible schooling.[27] As discussed in the first chapter, schooling in the colonies provided the only route for upward social mobility, and whilst it remained an inaccessible route for many, those who could access a full education were able to climb up the class hierarchy. In Britain, Black children's educational prospects were doubly impaired by the class structure of schooling and racial discrimination; 'working-class people were intended for working-class jobs – but Black working-class school leavers were not programmed for any jobs at all'.[28] For supplementary school initiatives in Britain, then, a key focus was to safeguard Black children's futures. Alongside this, as precursors to the current movements around abolitionist pedagogy in teaching and efforts to 'decolonise' the curriculum, community initiatives such as the Gresham Project worked to repair what Bernard Coard had called the 'conditioning effect' of mainstream education on Black children. Through school, Black children were conditioned to accept that 'all the great men of history were white', and thus the Black movement was tasked with undoing this narrative.[29] Accordingly, as with many other supplementary schools and Black-led youth centres that emerged during this era, the Gresham Project placed importance on encouraging young people to engage with Black histories and cultures, to empower them as people of African descent. It outlined its general aims thus: 'It is normally concerned with the specific problems of black people of all ages; but principally with those of black youngsters in the recreational, educational, informational, and other areas'.[30] This focus was similarly the case for other supplementary education projects that were developed by Black political groups, including at New Beacon Books' George Padmore Supplementary School and the Black Liberation Front's Headstart Supplementary School, both based in North London; and the Abasindi Saturday School run by the Abasindi Cooperative, a Black women's organisation based in Moss Side, Manchester.

In 1973, the Gresham Project's first year, they carried out a
summer project in August with various activities for local young
people, including a reading group, remedial English lessons, excur-
sions, a barbeque, puppet shows, and film screenings. The selection
of films included popular movies of the time such as *Hard Contract*
(1969), and *Cat Ballou* (1965), as well as the more political choice
of *Madina Boe* (1968).[31] The latter was a Cuban documentary
filmed in the liberated areas of Guinea Bissau during its war of
independence from Portuguese colonialism. Gerlin and other
organisers of the project were keen to weave in political education
within the project's activities. Although it was a political project
by nature, the supplementary school movement by and large was
not solely concerned with Black liberation and radical politics. But
those schools and youth projects that were led by radical activists
found deliberate ways to instil revolutionary politics in both the
educational and recreational activities.[32] The summer project was
regarded a success, with some participants who had been previously
labelled as 'remedial' by their schools subsequently being praised
for their 'excellent academic performance' in the aftermath of the
programme. Gerlin was one of five people to receive a commen-
dation for the summer project's success.[33] The summer projects
continued in the years that followed and included trips outside of
London to the countryside and seaside, which allowed the young
people involved to gain new experiences outside of their inner-
city environment. As Gerlin recalled, the programmes of activities
that Gresham Project and its summer projects bolstered the young
people's sense of self and gave them experiences that would not
otherwise have been available to them. Simultaneously, Gerlin was
gaining the respect of her wider community for her practical rather
than rhetorical approaches to activism:

> Because they were labelling our children as Educationally
> Subnormal, we set up Saturday Schools, and we had Summer
> Schools. We took the children out to different places, because
> their parents couldn't afford to take them and we took them
> to the seaside once, Brighton, they were so happy those kids.
> Because they never saw the expansive water before, and they
> could get in it. We did a lot of community work, commu-

nity development. All the time we were involved at different levels, so the people respected us because we weren't just talking or shouting, we were also protecting, working with the children and teaching and training them and bringing back some of their culture to them. We would have people who would come in and talk to them about the Caribbean, Africa.[34]

Although they had slightly different responsibilities on the Project, Gerlin and Ansel frequently combined forces to solve crises their young people were facing. They often found themselves intervening in these crises to veer their young people away from potentially harmful situations. The Gresham Project, with its close proximity to Brixton Police Station, played a particular role in de-escalating situations involving the police and young Black people. Both Gerlin and Ansel had previous experience to draw from in different contexts. Gerlin was arriving on the Project from having developed the Seventies Coffee Bar in Paddington, while Ansel found his way to Gresham after having taught English and Liberal studies at Sydenham Girls School. Whilst at Sydenham, Ansel had developed a rapport with the students of African and Caribbean descent, and organised activities which helped them to explore their cultural identities and find common ground with each other.[35] A large part of Gerlin and Ansel's work at Gresham was related to the task of keeping the young people away from the courts. While the police were actively discriminating against young Black people, some of them – having been miseducated by the school system, facing limited job prospects and criminalisation of their identities – were engaged in illegal activities. This of course set them in greater opposition with local police, and made the Gresham Project a hub of safety in an otherwise hostile location. Engaging in criminalised activities could be seen as a method of resistance to the oppressive systems young people were facing.[36] As Paul Gilroy and others have argued, criminalised activities can take on symbolic meanings, and in any case, those activities that are considered illegal are 'elastic and the limits of the law have been repeatedly altered by intense class conflict'.[37] All of these factors complicated Gerlin and Ansel's work. As Ansel recalled:

[Gresham] had a particular relationship to the police station because of the young people going there – always confrontational. Also, at the time, there was this moral panic about mugging because it was very prevalent at the time in South London. For some reason, Gresham Project ... attracted a lot of those young people. And I confess, a lot of them were involved in criminal activity, but we were working with them. Interestingly, around that time, the revolutionary justification for that was like it was a deliberate liberation, taking away from the people who were opposing you, so therefore it wasn't theft.[38]

In order to steer these young people away from petty crime, Gerlin and Ansel had to provide them with knowledge and experiences of viable alternatives. Gerlin began to build a reputation for how she approached these situations:

One seminal experience I had was when Gerlin and I went and spoke to a few of the girls, and our goal was to say, 'Come on, come back with us. We'll take you back to school'. And one of the girls went into her pocket and pulled out a wad of money. She said, 'What do you want me to do, go back to school to pack the shelves of Woolworths? Look at what I've made in less than half a day'. And that threw me back because I didn't have the proper answer for that, I couldn't motivate anybody else beyond that. And it took me a while. And that's how Gerlin was important. We would come back and we would think things through and discuss it, and develop strategies for that. And that was her strength – she can see the broad picture.[39]

One of Gresham's regular attendees was Janet Morris, who was a student at Brixton College at the time and used to frequent the centre alongside other college friends. She asserted that the project 'basically gave us an identity', and recalled that some of their activities included attending marches, receiving visits from activists such as Darcus Howe and Paul Boateng, and visiting other youth centres across England including in Liverpool and Manchester.[40] Janet credited Gerlin with advising her on writing her CV and encouraging her to apply for a job with Lambeth Amenities, stating that 'Gerlin had a way about her, very calm. She helped to push you'.[41] Janet was successful in her job application and became Lambeth's youngest Black Senior Officer.[42] Building on her experience from the Seventies Coffee Bar in opening up a space to explore the specific issues facing Black girls, Gerlin was similarly concerned with the discourse around women's rights in the Black movement more broadly. In July 1973 *Race Today* ran an article entitled 'Unmarried Black Mothers: Problems and Prospects'. This article aimed to tackle the lack of appreciation on the gendered dimensions of alienation felt by Black youth in Britain generally: 'Seldom, if ever, is the social violence inflicted on black youngsters examined or reported – and certainly not the violence that young black girls hardly out of their teens are subjected to'.[43] The article traversed some of the pertinent topics relating to Black girls, most notably the lack of support for young single mothers by the State, as well as poor treatment and attitudes directed at them by Black men and the wider community. The following month's issue of *Race Today* printed a response to this article from Gerlin, who praised the article's description of the pervading attitudes of State institutions toward young Black girls, but critiqued its failure to make mention of girls' experiences of abuse at Social Security offices. Her response highlighted her expertise on this area due to her job role, which put her in close proximity to young girls with lived experiences of these issues:

Sir,

In the article on Unmarried Black Mothers: Problems and Prospects which appeared in last month's *Race Today* your reporter described clearly the attitudes of different local government and social agencies to these girls. However, there is one aspect that was not brought out enough.

My work brings me into close contact with single black mothers and the thing that they complain about most is the treatment given to them at Social Security offices. The degrading questions and harassment they get from the officials needs looking at, not least because it adds greatly to the frustration the girls already feel.

Gerlin Bean,
Gresham Project,
1 Gresham Road,
London SW9.[44]

As Gerlin's mentorship skills advanced during her time at the Gresham Project, so did her credibility among others in Brixton. She became known as a woman of action. And in demonstrating her commitment to young people, she attracted the attention of other key activists, some of whom became collaborators in the major project of building one of the first autonomous Black women's organisations: the Brixton Black Women's Group (BBWG). Two of these women, Olive Morris and Zainab Abbas, initially met Gerlin via the Gresham Project in 1973, and co-founded the BBWG with her in the same year. Of the encounter with Olive Morris, Gerlin said:

> I didn't meet [Olive] until 1973 when I came to work at Gresham. And she heard, and she came one day riding her bicycle. Because she was like that, she always wanted to check you out and see who you are. So I met her and straightaway we developed this relationship in terms of we were on the same wavelength, more or less, and so that was very nice.[45]

Olive Morris had an impressive reputation of her own around Brixton. She was active in the Brixton chapter of the Black Panther Movement in her teen years, and gained notoriety due to her intervention during a police attack on a visiting Nigerian diplomat. On 19 November 1969, the diplomat parked his Mercedes car outside of the popular Desmond's Hip City record shop while his wife and children shopped inside. The police officers, seeing a Black man in an expensive car, wrestled the diplomat out of the car and broke his arm, prompting an immediate response from onlookers, Olive included. After shouting at the police to 'get off of' the man, Olive herself became the victim of police brutality. She was badly beaten, thrown into the back of a police van, separated from the other arrested women and sexually assaulted by a group of officers in a solitary cell. After reporting the details of this attack in the BPM's newsletter the event gained notoriety, as did Olive as a heroic local resident.[46]

Zainab, who had not long since moved to London from Birmingham, also met Gerlin at the Gresham Project.[47] Zainab had been active in the Afro-Caribbean Self-Help Organisation (ACSHO) in Handsworth, Birmingham, and hoped to transfer her activist work to London-based organisations. However, like Gerlin, Zainab was only interested in organisations that prioritised meaningful action and self-help projects: 'I was somebody who got on and did things, because to me, that was the positive side of activism'.[48] Having met Gerlin and Ansel, Zainab was able to make her entry into the core of the Black Liberation Front (BLF). In addition to her work with the BLF, she swiftly became involved in Brixton's activist scene and was taken under Gerlin's wing, staying with her for a while. From there, she met Olive Morris and Liz Obi, who were both active in the BPM at the time, and was invited to move into their squatted flat on Railton Road. Through these exchanges and the growing bonds between Black women activists, a substantial network began to take root. In addition to forging these local connections, Gerlin's work at Gresham also took her outside of her immediate community. Ama Gueye, a leading force in the East London Black Women's Organisation from its formation in 1979, traced her initiation into Black community activism back to a visit by Gerlin and Ansel to her university when she was a student in the mid 1970s. As a member of the University of Sussex's African Students Union during her studies, Gueye sat in the audience as Gerlin and Ansel addressed the Union as representatives of the Gresham Project, and called upon the students to volunteer to help disenfranchised young Black people. For Gueye, Gerlin remains a personal hero for the role she played in encouraging her and other students to direct their energies into the Black community, and later for her role in the course of events which led to the establishment of Black women's groups such as the East London Black Women's Organisation.[49]

In 1974, a year into its operations, the Gresham Project became the Abeng Centre. This redefinition marked an important point in the centre's trajectory, and produced challenges for the workers to 'legitimise its educational priorities and ideology'.[50] The centre's new name reflected the aim by workers to define the centre as rooted in the heritage of the community it served. Abeng is the name of a musical instrument made from cattle horn. Originating from the Akan people in modern-day Ghana, the abeng is an important symbol of resistance and self-identification in Caribbean history. The instrument was (and still is) commonly used by Maroons to communicate news and messages over long distances, without the content of these messages being intercepted by outsiders. The Abeng Centre hosted a daily drop-in centre for unemployed youth, work experience, career advice, as well as a schedule of adult classes on weekday evenings and supplementary school activities via Ahfiwe.[51] Soon a publication was produced, *AHFIWE: Journal of the AHFIWE School and Abeng*. It articulated the historical context under which the project first arose, as well as its aims:

> The impatience with which the community – black organi-
> sations, parents and churches – viewed the authorities'
> reluctance to deal positively with these issues led to the devel-
> opment of several Black supplementary schools. The Ahfiwe
> School is this just one such school serving the Black commu-
> nity in Lambeth.

> Our specific aims are:

> 1. To provide educational and vocational services for
>   Black youths to aid and stimulate a) their personal
>   development and b) their understanding and apprecia-
>   tion of the Black experience.

> 2. To encourage parents to be more closely involved with
>   and critically aware of the education system as it affects
>   their children, particularly in relation to employment
>   and further education opportunities.

> 3. To provide a range of supportive and advisory services
>   in order to negate the adverse social environment.

4. To develop in students the ability to think critically and politically so that they are able to analyse intelligently that which relates to their existence as an ethnic minority.[52]

AHFIWE not only served as a space for the Ahfiwe School and Abeng Centre to communicate its aims, activities and encourage the participation of others, it also served as a platform for local young people to publish their writings, which took many forms including testimonials, opinion pieces, political analysis, poetry and more. The Abeng and Ahfiwe School fostered a collective identity in the young people they catered to, and underpinning this collective sense of self was Blackness, as *AHFIWE's* slogan made explicit.[53] The Journal is a key source for understanding the methodologies that Gerlin, Ansel, and other active members of the Abeng Centre and Ahfiwe put into practice. The young people's contributions in *AHFIWE* were joined by adults who worked or volunteered their time at the centre. In this way, the centre presented youth and adults as equally capable producers of knowledge, although young people's work made up the majority of the publication. As *AHFIWE* expressed at the time, their works 'represent the feelings and perceptions of Black youths in Brixton – a voice that is becoming increasingly clear, loud and uncompromising'.[54] No surviving copies of *AHFIWE* to date feature writing credited to Gerlin, but many contributions from Abeng workers were anonymised. Gerlin's daughter Jennifer recalls her mother's work at the Abeng Centre as one of the more enjoyable aspects of her activist work to be involved with. As a teenager Jennifer frequented the Abeng Centre and contributed as one of its workers during an Easter half term. Her writing can be found in the second issue of *AHFIWE*, and consists of a reflection on the centre's Easter Project, which was conducted over a three-week period when she was fifteen. Her reflection highlights the hard work and long hours that the workers put into sustaining the centre, which she argued was not reflected in the pay they received:

The only thing that I found wrong with the project is that the work is hard and the hours are long, and I think that the

wages should fit according to the amount of work the workers
do but they do not. This does not mean that I would not work
for the same unfair sum again, because I think that it is very
necessary to keep the children occupied during the school
holidays especially in the area which the Gresham Project is
held and I think the project does this.[55]

It is well known that youth and community work is grossly underpaid in the UK, requiring long hours and hard work with little
resources to hand. Gerlin and other longstanding Black community workers were all too familiar with such difficult conditions,
and with making economic sacrifices to pursue work they knew
to be deeply important and necessary for the wider community.
According to Gerlin the lack of a decent wage didn't trouble her,
and she had little desire for material items. That being said, it's
clear that she suffered frequently from burnout and that her work
impacted her mental health. Responding to a question in her
Shrew interview about how her work 'meshed with' her private
life, she responded frankly: 'It's very difficult to fit in everything
I would like to do. I'm exhausted all the time – not so much
physically but mentally I feel drained'.[56] She was far from alone in
this; activists, community workers and those in caring professions
will know too well the toll that such work can take on mental
wellbeing. In the same conversation, which took place during
her time at the Seventies Coffee Bar, Gerlin detailed her weekly
expenditure and a rough breakdown of her costs. The similarity
of her role at the Abeng Centre means she was likely living within
comparable constraints:

> At the moment I seem to be overspending. I can live on about
> £10 a week quite easily but at the moment I'm living on about
> £20 a week ... I think half of it goes on food – even more than
> half because I hate cooking and I tend to eat out more than
> I eat in because of the hours I work ... clothes and makeup
> come least in my money.[57]

BRIXTON COLLEGE

In the late 1970s, having carried out important work with young people on improving their relationship with learning, Gerlin made the decision to advance her own education. She studied for a Social Science and Administration undergraduate degree at the London School of Economics (LSE).[58] LSE in this period was a hotbed of activity for radical students, who were able to forge connections with each other and organise within a multitude of political movements. Students and activists developed various radical political groups on the LSE campus, and Gerlin was involved with at least two of them. The first of these was the Gay Liberation Front, founded in an LSE classroom in 1970 (albeit before she was an LSE student).[59] The second, and the more substantive in terms of Gerlin's level of involvement, was the Organisation of Women of Asian and African Descent (OWAAD), which Gerlin co-founded in 1978 whilst a student along with other Black women activists, namely members of the Brixton Black Women's Group and the African Student's Union.[60] It was also at LSE that Gerlin met Gail Lewis again and invited her to join the Brixton Black Women's group.[61] After graduating Gerlin left her role at the Abeng Centre. Now armed with her Social Sciences degree, she took up the position of Guidance Councillor at Brixton College for Further Education. Located on Brixton Hill, the college has since been amalgamated into what is now South Bank Colleges. Gerlin worked alongside her long-time comrade Beverley Bryan, who worked first as an English lecturer and soon became the Head of the English department.[62] Gerlin and Beverley brought with them their philosophies on uplifting young people and the importance of educational experiences which nurtured a positive sense of self for Black students. They went about fostering this in the context of a mainstream educational setting in several ways. Conscious of the importance of broadening young people's horizons, Gerlin and Beverley took a group of students on a trip to Brussels in 1979.[63] They were both also concerned that even though a large proportion of the student population were Black, the staff population had only a handful of Black people. They set up a Black staff group, beginning with just the two of them as the first members, with the intention of pushing for a more representative staff body. As Beverley recalls, the staff demographics began to change substantially thanks to their efforts:

> We started a Black staff group. There was only a couple of us and the idea was to get the teaching population to look like the student population. So you move from 200 white staff and maybe three Black staff, and over the years you change the population so you might move to twenty-five to thirty, and the kind of tension is whether they actually made it any better for the student experience. You've got to think about who you're actually employing. We spent most of the time being very disciplined and made sure we did employ Black staff, we made sure we were represented on the panels. [64]

Their methodology in the staff group was to utilise an Equal Opportunities policy from the Inner London Education Authority, which stated that the Black community (alongside other marginalised groups) should be represented on interview panels, and that interviewees should be asked certain questions pertaining to racial equality to ensure staff hired were capable of relating to the students. The Black staff group was wholly successful in its aims; as Beverley recalls, by the time her and Gerlin left the college, 25 per cent of the staff population were Black, and eventually the college also had a Black Vice-Principle. [65] This transformation was evident long after they had parted ways with the college, and the methods that the Black staff group had pushed, drawn from the Equal Opportunities policy, remained ingrained in the college's recruitment processes. For example, Robin Landman (now CEO of the Network for Black Professionals), recalled his experience of getting a job at the college in 1986, which had a large number of Black staff by this time: 'You would walk into an interview and have twenty people in the room. Race equality people, gender equality, disability equality people, everyone was represented – I did a good interview and was offered the job'. [66]

Alongside the Black staff group, Gerlin and Beverley worked together to tackle an important issue for some of the college students: childcare. They requested funding from the Inner London Education Authority to establish a crèche for students who had difficulties juggling childcare responsibilities with their education. Clearly, the Inner London Education Authority was a useful tool for Gerlin and Beverley to carry out the changes they understood were required for supporting the needs of their students. The experience of working and organising together in a different context to their grassroots activism was also a significant bonding experience for them. As Gerlin recalled:

> We had a good time, we did things. We were innovative. We got the Inner London Authority to give us money to create a creche for the students who had babies and were coming to school and they had no childcare, so we provided that there in the college.[67]

Gerlin also developed a range of specifically youth-focused initiatives during her time with the Black Liberation Front. The BLF, based in northwest London, emerged in 1971 out of the north London chapter of the UK Black Panther Movement (BPM). The BLF was founded by several former BPM members who were either expelled or departed due to their concerns that it had become too dogmatic and stringently Marxist.[68] These activists believed the organisation required a refocus, and the BLF therefore defined itself as an organisation that put the needs of the Black working-class community in Britain at the forefront, and ensured to maintain its grassroots approach to Black radical activism. Like the BPM, and at least up until 1976, the BLF included some members of Asian as well as African descent, such as co-founding member and leading organiser Tony Soares. Others, such as Ansel whose Trinidadian roots include Afro-Caribbean and Chinese ancestry, Robert Singh, a Jamaican of Indian heritage, and Zainab, of Nubian Egyptian descent, were key members of the BLF and reinforced the idea that 'Black' as a descriptor as well as a politic encapsulated more than Caribbeans of African descent. This aspect of the BLF's position has been summarised well by Zainab: 'The attitude to our identity in the BLF was to encourage a holistic approach toward the concept of Blackness and all those people who were suffering. The concept of Blackness was based upon ideology as opposed to skin colour and so anybody who suffered from discrimination and was not white was Black'.[69] However, not all BLF members agreed on this, and the BLF's position was subject to change over the years depending on the influence of its members.[70] The BLF outlined its stance in the pages of its organisational newspaper, *Grassroots*: 'As a small minority in Britain, we cannot claim we will liberate the country or change its system. That is something the native working class must do for itself ... [Our] sole concern is survival for Black people in Britain and socialism in their homelands'.[71] The BLF supported the survival of Britain's Black community by producing various initiatives, drawing on the twin principles of self-help and self-reliance. As a part of this, the BLF developed the Grassroots Self-Help Community Project. This began sometime after the organisation's eviction from 54 Wightman Road and subsequent relocation to 61 Golbourne Road in Notting Hill, which took place in December 1972.[72]

Documentation pertaining to the Self-Help Community Project does not provide a concrete timeframe for its operations, but seems to suggest it was functioning in the financial year of 1973-1974.[73] Gerlin helped to cultivate the scheme alongside Ansel and BLF members Lu Garvey, Diana Anderson, Anthony Washington Nuney and Keith Bogle. In line with the BLF's general ethos, the Self-Help project, as its name suggests, was entirely run by BLF members and supporters on a volunteer basis. The project set up skills workshops in the basement of the BLF's new headquarters at 61 Golbourne Road. These workshops were facilitated by industry experts in vocations such as barbering, typesetting, and electrical repair. The costs incurred from the scheme were fundraised by the organising committee, which included Gerlin, and the committee members also contributed their own money in getting it off the ground. As the project outlined in a fundraising letter to supporters: 'Our success depends both on the extent of community involvement and our ability to be self-supporting'.[74] This letter suggests that the committee members struggled with juggling the task of fundraising within the community and simultaneously running the project. This gives some insight into the personal costs that youth projects required from organisers such as Gerlin. Other aspects of Gerlin's involvement with the Black Liberation Front (BLF) will be explored in more detail in the next chapter.

THE BRIXTON UPRISING OF 1981

As we have come to understand so far, protecting young people from police harassment and violence formed a large remit in Gerlin's community work, as one of the most pertinent issues affecting Black youth at the time. Here, it is necessary to recount Gerlin's work around policing in the run up to the Brixton uprising of April 1981, also commonly referred to as the 'Brixton Riots', which was the first of several uprisings across England in that year. The uprisings were a series of events that Black activists by and large, as well as concerned members of Britain's Black community – and indeed anyone paying attention to the state of 'race relations' – anticipated long before they took place. Gerlin had engaged in work prior to the uprising that had attempted to avoid the impending catastrophe. In the words of A. Sivanandan, 'the loom of British racism had been perfected, the pattern set. The strands of resistance were meshed taught against the frame. Something had to give'.[75] The 1981 uprisings were an explosive demonstration of young people's frustrations toward the incessant terrorism they experienced at the hands of the police departments in the various major cities across England. The Scarman Report, which was commissioned in the aftermath of the Brixton events, concluded that it was 'essentially an outburst of anger and resentment by young Black people against the police'.[76] In addition to an already tense relationship between police and Black youth, young people across England were also battling high levels of unemployment, poor housing conditions and a recession, which lasted from 1980-1982. It was estimated that at the time of the Brixton revolt, unemployment among Black youth was between 55-60 per cent nationwide.[77] On a local level in Brixton, 917,000 under twenty-five-year-olds were registered jobless.[78] Crowds took to the streets in the major areas of the country in which Black residents were concentrated, and where urban deprivation and police harassment was most rife. These areas included Brixton in London, Handsworth in Birmingham, Chapeltown in Leeds, Toxteth in Liverpool and Moss Side in Manchester. A year earlier, in April 1980, rioting had broken out in the St Pauls area of Bristol, and served as a precursor for what was to come on a smaller scale.[79]

In all of these areas, although the militant reactions of young people to their material conditions had been spontaneous, there were specific events which ignited the flames. In Brixton there were perhaps two major events which explain not why the uprising happened, but why the area erupted when it did. First, the death of thirteen Black teenagers (and a later fourteenth) in a house fire caused by a racist arson attack during a birthday party in New Cross, which came to be known as the New Cross Massacre.[80] The absence of any kind of support from the Thatcher government, the mishandling of the police investigation, and the distortion of facts by the mainstream media, culminated in the largest ever Black demonstration in British history, the Black People's Day of Action, on 2 March 1981.[81] The Black People's Day of Action saw 20,000 people walk from New Cross towards the Houses of Parliament and Fleet Street, the heart of the mainstream newspaper industry. The atmosphere of the march has been remarked on by many attendees; photographer Kevin Williams recalled 'the day's historic significance, as over 20,000 Black people arose, empowered, and marched peacefully through central London'.[82] Upon reaching Fleet Street, the demonstrators were met with swathes of police mounted on horses and kettled. As David Olusoga later set out, both the New Cross Massacre and the Black People's Day of Action confirmed to Black people in Britain that the ruling elite 'had no interest in the deaths of Black people', or in empathising with their lived experiences for that matter.[83]

The second major source of tension for Brixton's youth was the antagonistic action of the Metropolitan police just one month on from the Black People's Day of Action, coded 'Operation Swamp'. In this ten-day project, 150 plainclothes Met police officers descended on the area and conducted around 1,000 stop and searches and 150 arrests.[84] From 6-11 April, according to police records, 57 per cent of recorded stops were conducted on what they categorised as 'Negroid types', a racist term for people of visible African or Caribbean descent.[85] The official justification for Operation Swamp had been that crime in Brixton was particularly out of control and required a radical solution. What followed worsened the relationship between police and the community, providing a free-for-all for police harassment. One former constable, Peter Bleksley, recalled his time in

Brixton in the build-up to the eruption: 'I didn't join the police as a racist, but while I was in the police I became one. We just went out and made a bee-line for whosoever you wanted to arrest ... people had no chance of proving their innocence. Evidence was planted, that was a common practice. And assaulting people was an almost daily occurrence'.[86] In 1977, three years prior to the eruption, plans began for the establishment of a liaison committee in Lambeth, with the aim of providing a line of communication between the local community and police, and a platform for community groups to feedback criticisms and observations to the police about their activities. The driving force behind this project was the Council for Community Relations in Lambeth (CCRL). Its aims, as outlined below, were in a similar vein as Gerlin's own community work, in that they related to supporting local people and promoting equal treatment and opportunities, but from a non-radical perspective, as might be expected from a local council project:

i) To advance the education of the inhabitants of Lambeth without distinction of sex or race, or of political, religious or other opinions ...

ii) To promote and organise cooperation in the achievement of the above purpose and to that end bring together in council representatives of the statutory authorities and volunteer organisations engaged in furtherance of the above purposes within the borough of Lambeth.

iii) ... To advance the education of the inhabitants concerning good citizenship in a multi-racial society and the intellectual, artistic, economic and cultural background of the inhabitants of Lambeth. The council shall be non-party in politics and non-sectarian in religion.[87]

Despite its political neutrality and proximity to mainstream politics, Gerlin was a leading member of the CCRL for a time, and served as the chairperson of its Executive Committee.[88] By this time Gerlin was a highly regarded figure in the area, having earned her reputation through the various community initiatives she was involved with. Her commitment to advocating for the local community, and the most marginalised groups within it, likely prompted her to want to influence Lambeth Council's handling of issues that impacted them. The first attempt at a liaison committee didn't last long. An inaugural meeting was convened on 30 October 1978 and the committee ran into obstacles almost immediately after, due to the police's refusal to disclose its planned activities in the local area.[89] For example, the Met police's infamous Special Patrol Group (SPG) arrived a week later for a month's tour in Brixton and failed to announce this to the CCRL. When questioned about this decision later, Met Commander Adams made clear the intentions behind their surprise appearance: 'No good general ever declares his forces in a prelude to any kind of attack'.[90] Ironically, one of the SPG's official aims were to prevent outbreaks of public disorder, but in practice acted as an enforcer of violence. For example, in April 1979 during an anti-racism protest in Southall, London, activist and teacher Blair Peach was killed by an SPG officer.[91] This gives us some indication into the difficulties Gerlin was up against within the CCRL. As a radical and seasoned activist, Gerlin would have been all too aware of the fruitlessness of the Executive Committee's attempts at negotiating with an entity which viewed itself as an occupying force to be used against working-class citizens. In February 1979, three members of the CCRL were arrested by plain-clothes police officers for wearing sheepskin coats, which the police alleged were worn by suspected assailants in an earlier crime.[92] One piece of evidence that provides us with some insight into Gerlin's contributions to the liaison committee is a letter written by her to the leader of Lambeth Council, Ted Knight, on 15 February 1979. As the CCRL's Executive Committee chairperson, Gerlin wrote to inform Knight of the arrests of CCRL members to illustrate the dire situation of the liaison committee, and to explain the committee's reasons for ceasing activity:

> We have now reached an impasse in police/community relations in Lambeth which, regretfully, will have serious ramifications for the future well-being of all our citizens. The police in [Lambeth] continue to show an increasingly flagrant disregard for people's rights and dignity and their

utter contempt for Black people was vividly demonstrated by their disgraceful and unlawful acts on innocent officers of the CCRL.

Without wishing to be alarmist, it must be stressed that the situation is grave and deteriorating daily. Unfortunately, our methods of trying to bridge the gap through dialogue have failed because the police responded to our efforts with resounding contempt. In the past we have come under enormous criticism for trying to achieve improved liaison through consultation and dialogue. As one atrocity after another unfurls, the police continues to blame the community, especially the Blacks and we have to admit, with much regret, that we reached the end of that road, having got nowhere.[93]

In this letter, Gerlin also strongly suggested that, in light of the liaison committee's stagnation, and without sign of any productive intervention from the government, the situation was rapidly escalating toward an impending crisis, which would likely take the form of an insurrection:

The Home Secretary has, not unexpectedly, rejected claims for a Public Inquiry into relationships between the police and Black people in Lambeth.

Where do we go from here? How can this serious matter now receive urgent attention at the highest level to avert the inevitable recriminations and violent confrontations which will inflict irreparable damage to all our people?[94]

In the last section of the letter Gerlin, on behalf of the executive committee, recommended that Lambeth Council organise a Public Inquiry, 'in the hope that documented evidence produced from such an Inquiry might move us forward into a new positive direction'.[95] In accordance with this suggestion Lambeth Council set up the Working Party for Community/Police relations in Lambeth. Through this Working Party the CCRL attempted to bring together different sections of Lambeth's community, by having each section represented in its committee. To that end, Gerlin and south Asian community activist Amrit Wilson sat on the committee as representatives of Black and Asian communities.[96] Although she had been instrumental in encouraging the formation of the Working Party, it is difficult to locate much evidence of Gerlin's involvement after it was established. Its overarching task was to collect evidence about the excessive use of stop and search powers by police, and to present findings on the overall state of relations between police and the community. Brenda Kirsch, who sat on the Working Party's committee as a representative of the trade union movement, recalls that Gerlin's involvement declined over the time of its activity, and that she was not often present at group meetings. Kirsch assumed that Gerlin had reservations about being involved with the project, likely due to it being a council-affiliated project.[97] There is also the likelihood that Gerlin's experience in the CCRL made Gerlin aware of the limitations of an endeavour like the Working Party, and the risk that the work could be in vain if not taken seriously by the police and government. In January of 1981, just three months before the Brixton uprising, the Working Party published its findings in a report.[98] It served as one of the most convincing pieces of evidence that such an uprising was by this time imminent. Like the CCRL's liaison committee before it, the police refused to participate in the Working Party's inquiry. It consisted mainly of evidence of police brutality, excessive use of stop and search powers, and community testimonies that all pointed toward complete distrust and resentment toward the police. The report detailed examples that Brixton's community, especially its Black youth, were already too familiar with. Such examples existed on a spectrum, from details of impolite attitudes from police officers toward citizens to breaking down the doors of privately owned homes in unauthorised searches, brutal treatment of suspects, and a disregard toward protocols for dealing with minors and young suspects.[99] Despite the importance of the Working Party's report in highlighting the severity of the situation in Brixton, it was largely ignored by those in positions of power. Its significance was also later overshadowed by the Scarman Report, which was commissioned by the government on 14 April 1981, days after the Brixton uprising.[100]

In response to the uprising, local community and political groups came together to form the Brixton Defence Campaign

(BDC), an ad-hoc committee. Its driving forces were the Brixton Black Women's Group (BBWG) and, secondly, Black People Against State Harassment (BASH). They were also joined by West Indian Parents Action Group (WIPAG), Organisation of Women of Asian and African Descent (OWAAD), Asian Women's Group, and Muhammed Ali Sports Centre. Later on, the *Race Today* collective also became involved. The BDC utilised the Abeng Centre as its base.[101] As we know, Gerlin was heavily involved in the majority of these projects and organisations, highlighting the degree of her activism and intertwined nature of the activist landscape at this time. The BDC's overriding aims included: to fight for the full legal representation of those arrested during the uprising, for the dropping of all charges due to the fact that the uprising was a legitimate protest against racist policing, to encourage a widespread boycott of the Scarman Inquiry and to continue mobilising the community against police brutality and State oppression.[102] It's difficult to discern Gerlin's level of involvement in the BDC, although certainly she would have been involved via her association with the BBWG, BASH, WIPAG, and the Abeng Centre. The BBWG's leading role in the BDC has been documented, but much like many other facets of the history of Black activism, there have been challenges to the historical accuracy of this, and former BBWG members have had to reassert the group's centrality to the BDC's activities. This was discussed in a recent interview between former BBWG members in 2022, which Gerlin would not have been able to participate in:

Monica Morris: During the Brixton Uprising, we did a lot of work locally, such as the Brixton Defence Campaign, which we started off leading. There were others around, such as Race Today, but we chaired the meetings, we did a lot of work in the Law Centre defending the people arrested during the uprisings as well as mobilising the community.

Suzanne Scafe: I think it's important to say that although men and women were involved in the Defence Campaign meetings, it was BWG who led the campaign. We were the organisers, the strategists, and we were the ones who made that connection with Brixton Law Centre and the Legal Defence Campaign, and organised the note-taking in the courts.

Monica: I'm really glad that we're having this conversation, because history is written by those who decide they are going to write it-

Beverley Bryan: -And often just by men!

Monica: Exactly! I remember seeing something that situated Race Today as being central to the Defence Campaign and that was not my recollection at all. How did we let this happen?[103]

The central role of the BBWG in the BDC is confirmed by the archived documents from the campaign. For instance, a letter inviting people of the community to attend the BDC's first public meeting, scheduled on 7 June 1981 and held at the Abeng Centre, was written and signed off by Suzanne Scafe, a member of BBWG, on behalf of the BDC.[104] Both the example of Gerlin's hesitancy towards the CCRL's Executive Committee and the collaboration between the BBWG and other community groups in the BDC call attention to the difficulties in cross-section organising, and bring up the nuances, contradictions and tensions within community defence projects. As reported by Jan Mckenley, an activist in the Black Women's Movement, the BDC was not exempt from these tensions: 'Quite a lot of groups came together to form this Brixton Defence Campaign, it was probably one of the first times there was a coalition. And it was uneasy you know, it wasn't easy to work ... although everybody knew each other, you chose your group for a reason, and the people who were in *Race Today* weren't always friendly with the people in the Defence campaign'.[105] These tensions are manifest in the conflicting accounts of who was most proactive in the campaign, and an ongoing battle for visibility of the contributions made by each group. Despite these challenges, the BDC was successful in its aim to raise £10,000 to pay for legal fees and fines for defence cases connected to the uprising.[106]

As we have seen, Gerlin's youth-centred activism was wide-ranging, spanning several arenas. Her activities as a youth worker, first at the Seventies Coffee Bar and then the Gresham Project/Abeng Centre, exemplify her work in communities at a grassroots level, where her interventions with young people's personal and familial issues, as well as their experiences with police, were most direct. Meanwhile, working in a mainstream educational setting like Brixton College provided Gerlin with an opportunity to improve the learning conditions of the college students, while also positively impacting the recruitment of Black staff. Although she experienced some discomfort in working on more apolitical, institutional projects, as her gradual evasion of the CCRL and its Working Party highlights, she made indelible contributions to them through her urgent calls to defend the welfare of the local community in Lambeth, and the young Black residents of Brixton in particular. Her collaborations with other activists such as Beverley Bryan, Ansel Wong, Gloria Cameron and others serve as an important example not only of Gerlin's tireless commitment to supporting, protecting and defending young Black people besieged by state violence, but also of the robust network of Black activists that existed during the 1970s and into the early 1980s. It was networks such as these that laid the groundwork for present efforts to transform education for young people in Britain; the ongoing struggles to decolonise the curriculum and reimagine education as a tool for liberation can be seen as outcomes of earlier struggles by Gerlin and other activists to provide young Black people with safe spaces for self-exploration and learning.[107] Gerlin and other concerned Black activists were also acutely aware of the intensifying and uncompromising violence of the British State, and actively sought methods for defending young people against this, in tandem with their youth work. Gerlin was passionate about creating a more equal society for younger generations, but also creating spaces where young people themselves could carry this struggle forward.

NOTES

1   Gerlin Bean, 'The Heart of the Race: Oral Histories of the Black Women's Movement', Black Cultural Archives: ORAL/1/3, 2009, p16; p33; hereafter BCA.

2   Enoch Powell, 'Rivers of Blood' speech, Birmingham, 20 April 1968, https://anth1001.files.wordpress.com/2014/04/enoch-powell_speech.pdf.

3   Peter Fryer, *Staying Power: The History of Black People in Britain*, Pluto Press: London, 2018, p387.

4   Amelia Gentlemen, 'The racist legislation that led to Windrush', www.theguardian.com, 29 May 2022.

5   Kehinde Andrews, 'Back to Black: Black Radicalism and the Supplementary School Movement', PhD thesis, University of Birmingham, 2010, p116; John Solomos, *Black Youth, Racism and the State: the Politics of Ideology and Policy*, Cambridge University Press: Cambridge, 1988, pp51-118.

6   Sally Tomlinson, *Race and Education: Policy and Politics in Britain*, Open University Press: Maidenhead, 2008, p30.

7   For more information on the SUS law and resistance to it, see https://fightingsus.org.uk/.

8   Bean, op cit, p16.

9   Bernard Coard, *How the West Indian Child is Made Educationally Sub-normal in the British School System*, New Beacon Books: London, 1971, p33.

10   Coard, op cit, p36.

11   For a more in-depth account of the Black Supplementary School Movement see Jessica Gerrard, *Radical Childhoods: Schooling and the Struggle for Social Change*, Manchester University Press: Manchester, 2014.

12   'Open Municipal Coffee Bar – Councillor', *Kensington Post*, 22 December 1961.

13   'Council coffee bar scheme', *Marylebone Mercury*, 16 June 1967.

14   '"Municipal" discotheque for the Harrow Road', *Marylebone Mercury*, 20 September 1968.

15   Gerlin Bean, 'No, we didn't burn our bras' in Hilary Robertson-Hickling (ed), *That Time in Foreign*, Hansib: London, 2016, p151.

16   Ibid, pp151-152.

17   Ibid, p152.

18   Gail Lewis interviewed by the author, 17 May 2023, p1.

19   Gerlin Bean interviewed in *Shrew*, 1971, p10.

20   Bean 2016, op cit, pp152-153.

21   Ibid, p153.

22   'Court story of punch up outside youth club', *Marylebone Mercury*, 10 November 1972.

23   Ibid.

24   'Youth put boot in – Magistrate', *Marylebone Mercury*, 1 December 1972.

25 An account of the Gresham Project's emergence can be found in Gloria Cameron, *Case Dismissed: An Ordinary Jamaican Woman; an Extraordinary Life*, Hansib: London, 2015, pp128-131.

26 The Bishop of Dover, 'The Revd Anthony Ottey', www.churchtimes. co.uk, 27 August 2021.

27 Paul Warmington, *Black British Intellectuals and Education: Multiculturalism's Hidden History*, Routledge: London and New York, 2014, p55.

28 Brian W. Alleyne, 'Anti-Racist Cultural Politics in Post-Imperial Britain: The New Beacon Circle', first published in Richard J.F. Day, Greig De Peuter, Mark Coté (eds), *Utopian Pedagogy: Radical Experiments Against Neoliberal Globalization*, University of Toronto Press: Toronto, 2007, pp207-226.

29 Coard, op cit, p31.

30 A.X. Cambridge and Cecil Gutzmore, 'Report on the Gresham Summer Project', BCA: WONG/2/6.

31 Ibid.

32 Kehinde Andrews, *Resisting Racism: Race, inequality, and the Black Supplementary school movement*, Institute of Education Press: London, 2013, pp35-36.

33 Ibid.

34 Gerlin Bean 2009, op cit, p9.

35 Ansel Wong in conversation with the author, 15 April 2022, p4.

36 Paul Gilroy, 'The Myth of Black Criminality', *Socialist Register*, 1982, pp47-56; Cecil Gutzmore, 'Capital, "Black Youth" and Crime', *Race & Class*, Vol 25, No 2, 1983, pp13-30.

37 Ibid, p47.

38 Ansel Wong, 15 April 2022, p6.

39 Ibid.

40 Janet Morris in conversation with the author, 21 May 2023

41 Ibid.

42 Ibid.

43 'Unmarried Black Mothers: Problems and Prospects', *Race Today*, July 1973.

44 Gerlin Bean, 'Letter to the Editor', *Race Today*, August 1973, p226.

45 Bean 2009, op cit, pp1-2.

46 This event is explored in detail in Tanisha C. Ford, *Liberated Threads: Black Women, Style, and the Global Politics of Soul*, University of North Carolina: Chapel Hill, 2015, p148.

47 Zainab Abbas interviewed by the author and Hakim Adi, 1 April 2021, p14.

48 Ibid, p2.

49   Ama Gueye interviewed by the author, 19 August 2020.

50   Ansel Wong, 'Editorial', *AHFIWE: Journal of the Ahfiwe School and Abeng*, No 2, BCA: WONG/2/1.

51   The Bishop of Dover, op cit.

52   Ansel Wong, 'Foreword', *AHFIWE: Journal of the Ahfiwe School and Abeng*, No 1, BCA: WONG/2/1.

53   For more analysis on the methodologies present in Ahfiwe School, see Rob Waters, *Thinking Black: Britain, 1964-1985*, University of California Press: Oakland, 2019, pp147-152.

54   Wong, op cit, *AHFIWE*, No 2.

55   Jennifer Hussey in *AHFIWE: Journal of the Ahfiwe School and Abeng*, No 2, p8.

56   Gerlin Bean interviewed in *Shrew*, 1971, p10.

57   Ibid.

58   Bean 2016, op cit, p154.

59   Hayley Reed, 'The Gay Liberation Front's 50th Anniversary', blogs.lse.ac.uk/lsehistory/2020/10/28/the-gay-liberation-fronts-50th-anniversary, 28 October 2020.

60   Stella Dadzie interviewed by the author, 25 July 2019, p8.

61   Gail Lewis, 'The Heart of the Race: Oral Histories of the Black Women's Movement', BCA: ORAL/1/21, p9.

62   Beverley Bryan interviewed by the author, 7 March 2023.

63   Gerlin Bean and Beverley Bryan in a postcard to Stella Dadzie (undated); Bryan 2023, op cit.

64   Beverley Bryan, 'The Heart of the Race: Oral Histories of the Black Women's Movement', BCA: ORAL/1/8, p16.

65   Bryan 2023, op cit.

66   FE Week Reporter, 'Robin Landman, CEO, Network for Black Professionals', https://feweek.co.uk/robin-landman-his-story, 10 May 2013.

67   Bean 2016, op cit, p158.

68   Rosie Wild, 'Black Was the Colour of our Fight. Black Power in Britain, 1955-1976', PhD thesis, University of Sheffield, 2013, pp104-105.

69   Zainab Abbas, '"Black Footprints": A Trio of Experiences', in Hakim Adi (ed), *Many Struggles: New Histories of African and Caribbean People in Britain*, Pluto Press: London, 2023, p245.

70   Ibid.

71   'Editorial', *Grassroots*, Vol 1, No 2, July 1971, p2.

72   W. Chris Johnson, '"The Spirit of Bandung" in 1970s Britain: The Black Liberation Front's Revolutionary Transnationalism', in Hakim Adi (ed), *Black British History: New Perspectives from Roman Times to*

the Present Day, Zed Books: London, 2019, p133.

73 'Grassroots Self Help Community Project', c. 1973-1974, Institute of Race Relations: BLF file, 01-04-04-01-04-01-04.

74 Ibid.

75 A. Sivanandan, 'From Resistance to Rebellion', in *A Different Hunger: Writings on Black Resistance*, Pluto Press: London, 1982, p47.

76 Scarman Report referenced in Tony Jefferson, 'Policing the riots: from Bristol and Brixton to Tottenham, via Toxteth, Handsworth, etc', in *CJM*, Routledge: London, 2011.

77 John La Rose, *The New Cross Massacre Story*, New Beacon Books: London, 2011, p50.

78 BCA, 'Defend Yourself, Unity is Strength: the Brixton Defence Campaign (1981-1985)', www.bcaexhibits.org/brixtondefence/background.

79 Project Zazi, 'The St Pauls Riots', www.blackbristol.com/st-pauls-riots.

80 For a more in-depth account of the New Cross Massacre and the community's responses to it, see Carol Pierre, 'The New Cross Fire of 1981 and its aftermath', in Adi (ed) 2019, op cit, pp162-175.

81 La Rose, op cit, p7.

82 Kevin Williams, '2nd March 1981 – Black People's Day of Action', *History Matters Journal*, Vol 2, No 2, Spring 2022, p11.

83 David Olusoga, *Black and British: A Forgotten History*, Pan Macmillan: London, 2016, p516.

84 Jefferson, op cit, p8.

85 Recorded stops in Brixton division by Operation Swamp officers, 1981, BCA: UPRISINGS/1/5.

86 Peter Bleksley, 'The Battle for Brixton', BBC, 2006.

87 Council for Community Relations in Lambeth: Constitution, National Archives: HO 266/90; hereafter CCRL.

88 Gerlin Bean, letter to Ted Knight, 15 February 1979, National Archives: HO 266/90.

89 CCRL: Constitution, National Archives: HO 266/90.

90 Ibid.

91 For more information on Blair Peach, his murder and the subsequent inquiry, see David Ransom, *The Blair Peach Case: Licence to Kill*, Friends of Blair Peach Committee: London, 1980.

92 Zig Layton-Henry, *Race, Government and Politics in Britain*, Palgrave Macmillan, 1986, p244.

93 Bean 1979, op cit.

94 Ibid.

95 Ibid.

96 Brenda Kirsch interviewed by the author, 2 July 2021.

97   Ibid.
98   Final report of the Working Party into Community Relations in Lambeth, January 1981, National Archives: HO 266/68/2.
99   'Wanted: Political will', *Guardian,* 19 April 1981.
100 Brenda Kirsch interviewed by the author, 2 July 2021.
101 'Attend Public Meeting of Brixton Defence Campaign' poster, June 1981, BCA: MCKENLEY/3/1.
102 BCA, 'Defend Yourself, Unity is Strength: the Brixton Defence Campaign (1981-1985)', www.bcaexhibits.org/brixtondefence/initiation.
103 Former BBWG members interviewed by Jade Bentil in Milo Miller (ed), *Speak Out! The Brixton Black Women's Group*, Verso: London, 2023, pp362-363.
104 Letter from Suzanne Scafe on behalf of the Brixton Defence Campaign, BCA: Gutzmore/1/2/2.
105 Jan Mckenley, 'The Heart of the Race: Oral Histories of the Black Women's Movement', BCA: ORAL/1/24, p10.
106 BCA, op cit.
107 For an example of a contemporary project which addresses this, see the work of the Young Historians Project, younghistoriansproject.org.

4

How do you see the future?
Revolutionary politics

How do you see the future?

Bloody. For me personally there is a lot ahead for me to do.
I don't know where to start. It's just hard work ahead of me
for the future… I would like to get more involved in things
that are happening. In changes in society.[1]

Just as Gerlin was drawn toward youth and community work from
the late 1960s onwards, in the hopes of contributing to an alternative to the oppressive political, economic and social systems in
place, so too was she later drawn toward revolutionary politics. The
1960s, when Gerlin was in her twenties, was a decade of rapid social
change, political transformation and the emergence of influential
subcultures that challenged the status quo. The civil rights movement in the US, anti-colonial movements in Africa, opposition
to the Vietnam War, and the burgeoning women and gay liberation movements all coalesced to produce an intense revolutionary
atmosphere. These movements saw no signs of slowing down at the
turn of the next decade. Indeed, the 1970s seemed to be a decade of
unfinished business, with heightened frustrations over the tangible
societal change that was yet to emerge. By the close of the 1960s
Gerlin was now in her early thirties, and keen to involve herself in
the radical projects taking place in London. In the words of her
longstanding comrade Ansel Wong, as a politicised person in the
1970s 'you started to dip your foot into little things that were hap-

pening all around'.[2] It was in this context of the radical vibrancy of
the late 1960s and early 1970s that Gerlin grappled with the duality
of being a mentor to those younger than her as well as a participant
herself in movements for social justice. At the same time, Gerlin's
understanding of her own position in the struggle – considering
her racialised identity, sexuality, class and gender – evolved swiftly
during this period, to the point that she became a political theorist
in her own right. Perhaps for Gerlin the climate of this era made the
future both an exciting and daunting prospect, full of struggle and
potential for learning. This chapter explores the enclaves of revolutionary politics which Gerlin was involved in and her position
within them.

BRITISH BLACK POWER

From 1965 to 1967, a new phase of Black political expression began
to emerge in Britain. The call for 'Black Power' inspired African,
Caribbean and Asian communities in Britain to unite and mobilise against the second-class citizenship they experienced. It was a
transnational movement, with firm roots across the US, Caribbean
and indeed Britain. Although the US movement was a key source of
inspiration for people in Britain, the British Black Power movement
represented a continuation of earlier struggles that had been waged
by Black communities here. Rosie Wild, whose study of Britain's
Black Power movement remains the most comprehensive to date,
pinpointed four major elements that made up the ideology of Black
Power in Britain. These were: identity, community control, anti-
colonialism and internationalism.[3] These elements had been core
aspects of British-based Black activism since at least the late nineteenth century. But Black Power politics had a specific militancy and
stylish revolutionary vigour that exemplified the countercultures
of the 1960s and 1970s.[4] The appearance of militant civil rights
activist Stokely Carmichael at London's Dialectics of Liberation
Conference in July of 1967 has been referred to as the moment of
incitement, delivering Black Power politics to the British metropole.[5]
Carmichael popularised the term 'Black Power' in 1966 after being
arrested in Mississippi during a civil rights march, and in this same

year the Black Panther Party was founded in Oakland, California. Carmichael articulated Black Power as the need to 'reclaim our history and identity from the cultural terrorism and deportation of self-justifying white guilt'.[6] For Carmichael, and many others throughout the globe who embraced the concept of Black Power, Black Liberation was a project that required a complete departure from the terms of struggle put forth by (white) liberalism, and encapsulated by earlier years of civil rights organising.

Just a month prior to Carmichael's London visit, the Universal Coloured People's Association (UCPA) was founded in Notting Hill by Nigerian playwright Obi Egbuna, who shared a platform with Carmichael during the Conference. At the time of its founding, the term 'coloured' was already outdated and 'Black' was the newly reclaimed, empowering descriptor for New Commonwealth communities in Britain.[7] Despite its name UCPA was undoubtedly a radical organisation, and it adopted Black Power as its ideology in the aftermath of the Conference. In doing so, it became the first official Black Power organisation formed in Britain. It eventually splintered into several other organisations, creating a national Black Power network. Outside of London, too, in Birmingham, Manchester, Leeds, Liverpool, Nottingham, Sheffield and elsewhere, Black Power groups sprouted organically. Through organisational newsletters, solidarity campaigns, demonstrations, workshops and conferences, the various Black Power groups in Britain maintained contact with each other and exchanged political ideas.[8] Gerlin was influential in two of London's major Black Power groups, and it was from within the Black Power network that she began planting the seeds that led to the development of a Black women's movement. Her first contact with Black Power organising was the UCPA. In explaining her motivation for joining the UCPA, Gerlin pointed to her personal experiences of racism during her nursing career as a key factor.[9] The UCPA, like the Black Power movement, was acutely concerned with the conditions faced by Black and Asian workers. As much of Britain's Black population were concentrated in service industries such as the NHS, there was an emphasis on documenting the exploitation of Black health workers, namely nurses. As part of its remit to encourage Black workers to empower themselves through uniting and challenging

their oppressive conditions, the UCPA published a pamphlet entitled 'Black Nurses Unite!' The pamphlet drew on examples of the
way in which Black nurses were discriminated against, held back in
their professions, and manipulated by their employers:

> Over the last few months, we of the Universal Coloured
> People's Association, have received several complaints of racial
> discrimination against Black nurses in British hospitals. Many
> Black nurses are working under great stress and strain, owing
> to the racially prejudiced attitudes of many white co-workers
> and ward supervisors ...
>
> We have a report from a Black girl in Derby. This girl holds
> five GCE "O" Level[s]. She applied to a hospital in Derby to
> do a course of training leading to the SRN. The matron of the
> hospital conned this girl into doing the SEN instead. We are
> sure that there are many more cases of this type. In explaining,
> the matron told the girl that 'in future, British hospitals would
> only employ Black women to be trained as SENs'.[10]

Clearly, the UCPA perceived Black nurses and other hospital
workers as a potential vanguard for a mass movement of Black
workers in Britain. For those with direct experience in the profession, Gerlin included, this was a compelling rallying call. In the
pamphlet, the UCPA laid out a plan of action for attempting its
proposed unifying project:

> This nonsense must be resisted. But resistance can only be
> effective in unity of action. Black nurses must get together
> and organise themselves into a solid bloc. After this, the
> nurses must broaden their struggle to include all Black
> hospital workers. And finally, the struggle must include all
> Black workers in Britain. In the final analysis we are all at
> the bottom of this racist British society ... Black nurses and
> all Black hospitals join the Black Workers Co-ordinating
> Committee.[11]

As for Gerlin's time as a UCPA member, there is very little documentation. Exactly when she joined, and her level of involvement

in the UCPA, is undetermined. There is available information, however, on the UCPA's activities, which in turn provides us with some idea of the kind of work that Gerlin and other activists in the organisation may have been involved with. Regular activities included weekly discussion groups, lessons in political skills such as canvassing, duplicating, poster-making, anti-thug patrols, film screenings, public meetings, demonstrations, and the production of the UCPA's *Black Power Newsletter*.[12] Alongside these, there were also committees which focused on specific topics, such as the Black Workers Co-ordinating Committee, as detailed above, and a Black Women's Liberation Committee. The UCPA asserted its embrace of 'all such activities which will promote the emancipation of our sisters all over the world'.[13] Although women's liberation began as a priority on the UCPA's agenda when it was founded in 1967, by 1968 its *Black Power Speaks* newsletter included a 'women's corner' that was openly hostile toward women's liberation, and suggested that Black women had to choose between the two movements.[14] In tandem with the wider Black Power movement, the UCPA identified Western capitalism and imperialism as the root cause of the oppressions faced by people of African and Asian descent, both those located in Britain and in their homelands. Blackness became a politic rather than a reference to African heritage or skin colour: 'by the political slogan BLACK POWER we mean to draw a sharp line between ourselves, and our mortal enemy capitalism and imperialism and all those who support and benefit from this monstrous system'.[15] It wasn't long until the UCPA came to the attention of the Home Office and police, who were anxious about the momentous spread of Black Power and its capacity to inspire civil unrest both in Britain and across the Commonwealth.[16] The surveillance and persecution of leading figures, such as Obi Egbuna, challenged the functionality of the UCPA. Paired with this, internal conflicts splintered Britain's foremost Black Power organisation into several groups. In the words of Tony Soares who, like Gerlin, began his Black Power trajectory with the UCPA, 'there wasn't any particular class distinction or class consciousness' in the organisation.[17] Due to this shortfall in the UCPA's programme, the Black Panther Movement was established in 1968, which put more emphasis on Marxism. This in turn facilitated the emergence of

the Black Liberation Front in 1971. On 26 July 1970, in homage
to the Cuban Revolution, what was left of the UCPA's membership base transformed into the Black Unity and Freedom Party
(BUFP). This transformation was coordinated with the central aim
of reorienting the organisation into a more explicitly class-focused,
Marxist-Leninist and Maoist Black Power group.

THE BLACK UNITY AND FREEDOM PARTY

From here on, the BUFP's longstanding position was that the
class system was the primary source of oppression in society.
Accordingly, the BUFP encouraged Black people in Britain to see
the necessity for a class-based revolution if racism was to be demol-
ished. Its 'Long Term Programme', which featured in every issue
of its *Black Voice* newspaper, clearly articulated this position: 'We
recognise the necessity of class struggle and the absolute necessity
for the seizure of state power by the working class and the bringing
about of socialism'.[18] In the aftermath of the splintering of the
UCPA, an assemblage of organisations now made up the broad,
nuanced composition of Britain's Black Power movement. By virtue
of this expansion, there was now some level of choice for those who
wanted to become formally involved in the movement, especially
in London. Several factors informed an activist's choice regarding
which organisation they joined. Location was important – people
usually joined organisations in close proximity to where they lived
or worked. Additionally, members of organisations often extended
invitations to their social networks, meaning people were influenced by their circle of friends. Lastly, each organisation had slightly
different interpretations of Black Power. Some subscribed to more
socialist and Marxist-Leninist politics, others followed a culturally
nationalist and Pan-Africanist line inspired by figures such as Ron
Karenga in the US, while others embraced both of these branches
of Black Power. Naturally, as Gerlin pointed out, people joined
organisations that they felt matched their own outlook: 'We just
chose which we felt more aligned with'.[19] In surveying the landscape of Britain's Black Power movement, the BUFP is the most
obvious example of the class-conscious strain of Black Power that

existed in Britain. The organisation was opposed to Black cultural nationalist tendencies and emphasised the importance of viewing Black liberation as inseparable from the global class struggle. For Gerlin, the BUFP reflected her own ideals: 'I was more in-line with the socialist perspective than just a Black nationalist perspective'.[20] Tracing Gerlin's activities during the Black Power era offers an important opportunity for understanding where she saw herself on the spectrum of Black Power politics, and how this helped shape her activism in this period.

The key instigators of the transition from the UCPA into the BUFP were Alrick (Ricky) Cambridge, George Joseph, Sonia Chang, Emil Chang and Danny Morrell. Ricky was a member of the Communist Party of Great Britain (CPGB), and had worked closely with Claudia Jones as her assistant for the *West Indian Gazette* up until her untimely death in 1964. The *Gazette* was founded in 1958, several years after Claudia Jones's deportation from the US to London after persecution for Communist activities. On her role in nurturing his radical politics, Ricky attested to the fact that 'she was my mentor in the 1960s before she died'.[21] The political flavour he brought to the BUFP was influenced in part by what he had learned from her, as well as his own experiences of communist politics and organising. For example, from the outset, the BUFP had a clearly well-defined understanding of women's liberation and how issues of gender fit into the wider question of Black liberation and anti-imperialism. Claudia Jones was an early proponent of what came to be known as intersectionality, arguing for better recognition of the Black woman's unique position in the struggle as a triply oppressed group on the grounds of gender, race *and* class.[22] Her contributions to this theory are epitomised by her writings, in particular her 1949 article 'An End to the Neglect of the Problems of the Negro Woman', wherein she declared 'Negro women – as workers, as Negroes, and as women – are the most oppressed stratum of the whole population', and in addition to their unique position in society, 'are the real active forces – the organizers and workers – in all the institutions and organisations of the Negro people'.[23] Through participation in the Black Power movement, Gerlin and other activist women would come to intimately understand Claudia's arguments, and received regular reminders that – despite rhetorical suggestions of the importance of women's liberation in the overall revolutionary project – Black women's contributions were too often overlooked and undermined by male chauvinist tendencies in mixed gender organisations.

Gerlin was central to encouraging the BUFP's commitment to women's liberation. There is a tangible lineage of women activists influencing the direction of Black Power politics, both as inspiring figures from the past (in the case of Claudia Jones), and as leading members of organisations (in the case of Gerlin and her contemporaries). Despite the political compatibility between the BUFP and Gerlin on paper, she was only a member of the BUFP for a year.[24] But during her brief stint her contributions were significant, and she formed strong personal and political bonds with fellow BUFP activists, in particular Ricky Cambridge, which outlasted her time in the organisation. They would go on to have a romantic partnership and live together in Brixton for several years throughout the 1970s. During her involvement, the BUFP established its Black Women's Action Committee (BWAC), which published a pamphlet entitled *Black Women Speak Out!* Gerlin is currently the only known member of the BWAC, as well as being the Committee's founding member and one of its leading theorists. The pamphlet consisted of ten pages and includes essays which appears to have been originally published by the Black Women's Action Committee between October 1970 and May 1971. This pamphlet wove together several related themes into a rich political manifesto, energetically articulating the three main categories of oppression faced by Black women and what needed to be done to fight against them. First, it outlined the BWAC:

> The Black Women's Action Committee, of the Black Unity and Freedom Party was set up in April of 1970, who saw the need for Black women to get together to talk about their special problems and ways of solving them.[25]

One of the pamphlet's essays implied that one of the BWAC's activities included protesting against the concept of beauty pageants. The following statement had been published in October, and was distributed by the Action Committee 'outside places where "beauty contests" are held':

BLACK WOMEN we call upon you to stop participating in your own degradation. Reject the role of a mere vessel for pleasure and for making profit...

Black parents do not encourage your 'good looking' daughters into prostitution; beauty contests are just the first stop along this path.

A diploma in wig-making and applying cosmetics is useless and is a fake. There are no shortcuts – education is the only way to improve oneself.[26]

This hard-line message against Black women's participation in the beauty industry was synonymous with the Black Power movement's overall position on this issue. Black Power newsletters were often filled with calls for Black women to get rid of anything that represented Eurocentric notions of beauty, such as wigs, cosmetics and hair straighteners, and instead embrace their natural beauty. This echoed the 'Black is beautiful' movement, which encouraged Black women to wear their hair in its natural form and use the iconic afro hairstyle as a celebration of Black identity. It is of particular note that the BWAC were involved in protesting beauty contests in late 1970 given the events at the Miss World pageant of that year. On the 20 November 1970, the popular Miss World pageant was held in the Royal Albert Hall in London. Beginning in 1951, the Miss World pageants were highly publicised annual occurrences. From 1959 up until the 1980s, Miss World events were broadcast on the BBC and backed by multinational companies. With the women's liberation movement beginning to take shape by the late 1960s in Britain, women's liberation activists saw the 1970 pageant as the perfect stage for a large-scale protest against the objectification of women's bodies for patriarchal and capitalist consumption. The protest included pickets outside the venue, and sixty women infiltrated the ceremony to disturb proceedings with flour bomb attacks.[27] Not only were protesters riled by what they saw as the overall objectification of women that they witnessed during the ceremony, they were also angry at a series of racist jokes about the ongoing war in Vietnam by presenter Bob Hope.[28] As much as it was a site for controversy, the Miss World of 1970 included a historical first, when the Grenadian contestant Jennifer Hosten became the first Black winner in the pageant's history. It becomes all the more significant that the Action Committee would have been distributing their ideas on the participation of Black women in beauty contests during this historical event.

Another aspect of the *Black Women Speak Out* pamphlet was the inclusion of quotes by, and dedications to, notable revolutionary figures like Sojourner Truth, Mao Tse Tung, Madame Nguyen Thi Binh, Leila Khaled, Claudia Jones, and a sizeable list of US Black Panther women:

'We have all been thrown down so low that nobody thought we'd ever get up again; but we have been long enough trodden now: we will come up again ...' Sojourner Truth – 1853.[29]

'Everything reactionary is the same; if you do not hit it, it will not fall' – Mao Tse Tung.[30]

We salute and embrace all sisters who have escaped from their straightjacket role of being women in this capitalist society and have begun to start to think for themselves and are dealing deathblows to this murderous and oppressive system. We remember Claudia Jones ... We salute: Erika Huggins, Joan Bird, Frances Carter, Rose Smith, Loretta, Luckes, Margaret Hudgins, Maud Frances of the Black Panther Party; Angela Davis, Madame Binh, Leila Khaled. Free Kathleen Cleaver. Free all our sisters.[31]

In addition to honouring influential thinkers, both historical and contemporaries of the BWAC, the pamphlet also detailed the theorisations of the BWAC women themselves. As the only known member of the committee and founding member, we might safely assume that Gerlin played an important role in developing and expressing these ideas. These ideas represented the class-consciousness espoused by the BUFP in an essay entitled 'The oppressed of the oppressed':

Black women are the oppressed of the oppressed. They are oppressed as being part of the working-class, as being Black and as being women.

True equality between the sexes can never be achieved in a capitalist society for inequality based on national, racial and sexual differentials is an integral part of the mechanism of capitalist exploitation ...

Therefore, women must struggle to change this exploitative structure from its economic foundations thereby transforming the social relations which result... In the meantime, women must fight for equal pay and status at the point of production.

However, the struggle for freedom, by women, for women, cannot be separated from the world's anti-capitalist, anti-imperialist, workers movement – Black and white ... UNIFY THE STRUGGLE, STRIKE AT THE MAIN ENEMY![32]

From the 22-23 May 1971, the National Conference on the Rights of Black People in Britain was convened at Alexandra Palace, North London. To some it is remembered as the 'Black Power conference', considering it was organised by Black Power-oriented organisations and its agenda mirrored the topics and questions taken up by the British Black Power movement. Alongside groups such as the Handsworth-based Afro-Caribbean Self-Help Organisation (ACSHO), London's Black Panther Movement (BPM), Leeds-based United Caribbean Association and others, the BUFP was also active in the conference's proceedings. The idea of the conference seems to have stemmed from the BPM, and the organisation's de facto leader, Althea Jones-Lecointe, was one of the conference speakers. She also happened to be one of the only women in a visible leadership position of a Black Power group in Britain.[33] The two-day event opened with a play entitled 'The Black Experience', and sessions were delivered on a wide range of topics relating to the experiences of Black people in Britain. These included: Black youth issues; legal rights; self-defence organising; Black political prisoners; housing; education; employment; immigration; and Black women.[34] The BWAC delivered the contents of this pamphlet at the conference, and it soon provided the ideological basis for the Black women's movement. A transcript of the conference's discussions has not yet surfaced and therefore there is no evidence of who might have been involved in this session, or if Gerlin was in attendance. In any case, she evidently made an indelible contribution to

the direction of the discussion around Black women's issues via the
BWAC and *Black Women Speak Out.*

THE BLACK LIBERATION FRONT

The Black Liberation Front (BLF) was one of the longest standing
organisations that emerged out of the Black Power era. Set up in
early 1971, it remained active until 1993.[35] In the first issue of
the BLF's *Grassroots* newspaper, the editorial clarified its approach
as a community-oriented, non-hierarchical collective: '*Grassroots*
is not an ideological paper. It does not propagate any dogmas,
doctrines or isms. Its function is to serve the community. The
articles do not represent the views of the organisation. Anybody
is free to write in this paper'.[36] Alongside this accessible approach
to journalism, another thing that set the BLF apart from other
organisations in London was its dislike of publicity and its staunch
Pan-Africanism. The BLF was one of the key groups which
helped to organise the British delegation to the sixth Pan-African
Congress in Dar es Salaam, Tanzania, in 1974. By contrast,
the BUFP was not involved in such preparations, as explained
by former BUFP activist Lester Lewis: 'The BUFP could have
participated but it did not because it was not Pan-Africanist, it
espoused Marxist-Leninist, Mao Tse Tung thought'.[37] Gerlin
attended, alongside fellow BLF activists Zainab and Ansel.
Zainab, who worked primarily in the BLF's internationalist core,
recalled that in the early years of the group's existence, the BLF
built strong ties with liberation movements such as FRELIMO
in Mozambique, MPLA in Angola, SWAPO and SWANU in
Namibia, ZANU in modern-day Zimbabwe, and the ANC and
PAC in South Africa.[38] Alongside Zainab, whose partner Emil
Appolus was the official representative of the Namibian govern-
ment-in-exile for the United Nations, it was Tony Soares who was
largely responsible for forging these connections with the African
continent during a solo trip to Dar es Salaam in August 1971.[39]
To this day, the core group of activists who were around during
the BLF's most intensive years in the early 1970s maintain an air
of secrecy on the BLF's international activities.

Exactly what attracted Gerlin to the BLF is an interesting question. The details of her shift from the BUFP to the BLF are hard to decipher from her own oral history interviews, conducted almost forty years after the event, in which she referred to the BLF with a muddled chronology and appeared to mix up the two organisations. In her interview for *Shrew* published in September 1971, she confirmed that she was no longer a member of the BUFP and was now attached to another group in a different area, but with the same circle of activists: 'I used to go to something called the Black Unity and Freedom Party. That went on for a while and then it stopped. Then late last year some time I started up another group with the same people but in a different area'.[40] If we assume Gerlin's representation of time in her phrasing of 'late last year' is accurate, she would have departed the BUFP at least five months before the Alexandra Palace conference took place. What is more, the organisation she was referring to could not have been the BLF as it was not yet in existence, and there is no record of her having been involved with any other Black Power group other than the BUFP and BLF. We can definitively rule out the Black Panther Movement as the organisation she might have been referring to, as both Gerlin and others have attested she was never involved with the group.[41] We might consider the possibility, then, that Gerlin was merely estimating a timeframe of 'late last year'. While the BLF operated out of Wightman Road in Haringey, travelling from her work place in Harrow Road to BLF meetings and events would have only been marginally quicker than travelling to the BUFP's headquarters in Fairmount Drive, Brixton. It wasn't until the BLF's move to Golbourne Road in December 1971 that Gerlin's travel from work to BLF meetings would have been a short walking distance of ten minutes. Since we can therefore assume that distance was not a factor in Gerlin's motivation for relocating her energies from one organisation to the other, it was perhaps more likely the BLF's principles that led her to become involved. As an easy going and community-oriented person, it might be that the BLF's non-dogmatic methods of organising, community-oriented activities such as *Grassroots* newspaper, and the Grassroots Community Self-Help Project were more in line with her own principles than what she'd found during her time with the BUFP. Among friends and comrades, Gerlin was known for her ability to collaborate with a swathe of organisations, projects, and collectives, and was not as concerned about the ideological nuances that often led to divisions in the movement. Beverley Bryan attested to this:

> She moved to a lot of different organisations. She was never in the Panthers, but she spent some time in BUFP. And that's such a contrast between BLF and BUFP. Complete opposites on the spectrum. But she was quite embracing in that way, that she would not dismiss one group because they were not saying the right thing. As long as they were doing the work.[42]

As detailed in the last chapter, Gerlin also had a working relationship with one of the BLF's leading activists, Ansel Wong, from 1973, when they both started working at the Gresham Project. When asked whether he remembered how Gerlin got involved with the BLF, Ansel suggested that it was likely that their being colleagues played a role: 'I'm not sure how she got involved. But I certainly got involved, and I assume because we were so close working together, it was quite natural. She just fell into it'.[43] While Tony Soares recalled Gerlin being active in the BLF at one stage and very influential in the group, he couldn't recall exactly when she became involved, or how long she was an active member.[44] The BLF was also under regular surveillance by the Metropolitan Police's Special Branch division and subject to several raids on its premises. Mindful of the need to protect the privacy of its members, the BLF intentionally didn't keep membership lists or other records that might be compromised.[45] As a result, there's no documentation that can provide us with a concrete timeline of her involvement. But a rough timeframe can be produced using the testimonies of Gerlin and her comrades, as well as her presence in the Community Self Help Project and sixth Pan African Congress, to suggest she was involved with the BLF at least between the years of 1971-1974.

In comparison to the BUFP, the BLF was not as consistent in approaches to the topic of gender, and the organisation's relationship with women's liberation was not straightforward. Given that, by the time of her arrival into the BLF, Gerlin was already engaging in women's liberation politics, and was armed with the experience of constructing a women's caucus within the BUFP, it's worth considering what the BLF's own stances on gender issues were upon her entry and whether she contributed to the evolution of the group's perspective. *Grassroots* newspaper remains the most pertinent source for tracking the BLF's ideological developments over the years. The various articles it carried on the subject reveal that the organisation was at times suspicious of women's liberation, viewing it as the pursuit of white women. At other times the BLF offered a more considered perspective on women's liberation, and encouraged consciousness-raising on the subject for all its members and supporters. But being that the line of argument changed so frequently throughout the group's lifespan, we can surmise that the BLF's commitment to addressing gendered issues depended on who was involved at the time and their opinions on the matter. Of course, since *Grassroots* encouraged its members and supporters to write from their own perspectives rather than following an organisational line, the extent to which we can interpret the BLF's perspective from *Grassroots* articles is limited. Nevertheless, each *Grassroots* issue underwent editing by a BLF member and the organisation did not print articles that presented views contrary to what it stood for. As the leading figure and most active member of the BLF during its first five years of activity, Tony Soares recalled that there was a generally progressive attitude toward women's liberation among the collective: 'If you go by what we were saying, and the literature [we read], and what we believed in, I think we were strongly pro-feminist in the ideology of the time'.[46]

Grassroots included a regular Sisters Column, which was at times also referred to as the Women's Corner, from its third issue, published sometime in June/July of 1971. As was the BLF's practice, authors used pseudonyms or their initials to maintain anonymity, making it difficult to ascertain who was writing for this section. Over the years the Sisters Column became increasingly irregular. A Family Page was introduced in its place in 1978, which discussed topics such as parenthood, contraception and healthcare. Certainly in its early years, the Sisters Column reflected the wider discourse of the Black liberation movement at the time. At its debut in 1971, the Sisters Column presented a 'Message from a Black sister', written by Sister M. The article urged Black women to turn their backs on

Eurocentric beauty standards: 'Sisters, let's stop competing against each other, and get together … Get rid of our wigs, straightening of our hair, painting our eyes and lightening our skin'.[47] Alongside this, the author also made reference to the nature of the oppressed position of Black women in facing both racism and patriarchy: 'Sisters, we are fighting two battles, one against our men oppressors and the other for the freedom of our people'. This theory of a 'double jeopardy' experienced by Black women was a popular one within the movement, having been put forward by Frances M. Beal in 1969.[48] Beal was a political organiser who witnessed the birth of Black Power politics in the US as an active member of the Student Non-Violent Coordinating Committee (SNCC). Beal's motivation for writing on the oppressed nature of Black women came largely from witnessing the shortfalls of some male activists, in their subscribing to sexist and misogynist assumptions about women's capabilities in the movement. One of her methods for fighting these issues was to set up a women's chapter in the SNCC, the Black Women's Liberation Committee. Evidently, British-based Black Power activists were actively engaging with these kinds of writings, interpreting the theories, and utilising the established practices in their own organising context.

In the same issue of *Grassroots*, the 'community news' section announced plans for a women's meeting: 'Black sisters to meet on Monday 26th of July to discuss women's problems. Time 8pm'.[49] It was cryptic, not including the location of this proposed meeting. It was likely held at an activist's house, as most women's meetings were, which might explain the omission of an address. The lack of detail in the announcement also suggests the meeting was only open to those already in the BLF's network. This is the only instance where mention of a women's meeting was made in *Grassroots*. Women's caucuses within Black organisations like the BLF were largely advertised by word of mouth, as they were not yet autonomous organisations with their own publications. Many women became involved through being invited by established participants. One example of this is Gail Lewis's memory of being approached by Gerlin at an event held at the West Indian Students Centre (WISC), located in Earls Court, in 1971. The event consisted of a talk by Penny Jackson, the sister of George

Jackson, a highly regarded US Black Power figure as part of the incarcerated group of activists known as the Soledad Brothers. This was Lewis's first exposure to revolutionary Black politics and Gerlin sought to take Lewis under her wing by bringing her along to a Black women's meeting.[50] Early on in the Black Power movement, women's groups from different organisations met to discuss issues as a larger collective. This cross-organisational phenomenon constituted the early Black women's movement in Britain. A study group was formed, following a similar model to the Black Women's Action Committee that Gerlin set up in the BUFP. It became a network for Black activist women from different groups, as Gerlin explained: 'I was in another organisation, the Black Liberation [Front] ... The women from the Panthers used to come and join with us as women, and then we would invite other women who weren't really aligned to anything to these meetings'.[51] Following on from *Grassroots'* first coverage of women's issues, the next instalment of Sister's Corner reprinted excerpts from the Black Women's Action Committee's *Black Women Speak Out* pamphlet, in an article titled 'Some thoughts on Black Women's Liberation'.[52] This development came after the Alexander Palace conference, in which the *Black Women Speak Out* pamphlet was presented to an audience of several hundred people from across England. It is clear then that the work Gerlin and the first Black women's collective that she set up did to articulate the situation of Black working-class women in Britain resonated with women throughout the movement. However, the messages contained in *Black Women Speak Out* also roused the suspicions of those who saw the growing pivot towards Black feminist politics in the movement as a threat to autonomous Black organising.

In the autumn of 1971, in the *Grassroots* issue which immediately followed, the Sister's Column ran an article which strongly refuted the idea that women's liberation was the purview of Black women, merging quotes from two prominent Black American women writers. The first was an excerpt from a piece for the *New York Times* by Toni Morrison: 'What do Black women really feel about women's lib? Distrust. It is white and therefore suspect'.[53] The second excerpt consisted of a lengthy rejection of women's liberation by Ida Lewis, former editor of *Essence*, a US-based Black women's lifestyle magazine. Lewis argued against Black women becoming embroiled in 'a family quarrel between white women and white men'. Her opinion stemmed from a concern that Black women might be diverted from the struggle for Black liberation: 'If we speak of liberation movement, as a black woman I view my role from a black perspective—the role of black women is to continue the struggle in concert with black men for the liberation and self-determination of blacks'.[54] Indeed, the entire Sister's Column, in contrast to its earlier embrace of *Black Women Speak Out*, positioned itself against what Gerlin and other Black feminist women were working to create within the Black Power movement: spaces for Black women to explore their gendered experiences in relation to the wider struggle for Black liberation. It is clear then that even as Gerlin was sowing the seeds of an autonomous Black women's movement based on a burgeoning Black feminist collective consciousness, she was at times met with resistance from the wider movement. Some activists were not yet convinced that women's liberation and Black liberation were sites of struggle that could be taken up by Black women simultaneously.

THE BLACK LIBERATOR

Unlike the other projects Gerlin involved herself in, *The Black Liberator* was not a practical community initiative. It embodied the intellectualist strand of the Black movement, providing analyses of the historical and contemporary struggles of Black people. Founded in 1973 by Ricky Cambridge and Cecil Gutzmore, *TBL* described itself as a 'theoretical and discussion journal for black liberation'.[55] It played an important role in the movement, providing timely and meticulous writings on the various sites of Black struggle, from examples of industrial action and class struggles waged by Black people in Britain to extensive narratives on liberation struggles on the African continent, and reviews of relevant publications. Stella Dadzie, who wrote for *TBL* on occasion, as well as working with the collective in an administrative role and selling copies outside Brixton tube station, summarised *TBL*'s role thus: 'You need your theory. You need someone to step back and say, "What's happening? How does this relate to what's going on over here?" You need your theorists'.[56] Although Gerlin was fundamental to *TBL*'s production, her contributions were mostly indirect; she provided a physical production space, as well as constructive criticism and occasional editorial help. Ricky and Cecil were joined by Colin Prescod, activist, filmmaker and son of Tobagonian performer and cultural activist Pearl Prescod, as a consistent contributor to *TBL*. The journal quickly gained a reputation for its heavy theoretical jargon, and in this way stood in contrast to the style of writing found in the majority of Black community organisational newsletters, such as *Grassroots*. Although it was sold on street corners in a variety of areas, it was not an easily accessible paper to the 'ordinary' person. In an attempt to alleviate the issue of inaccessibility, Ricky provided a glossary of political terms at the end of each issue, to help guide the reader. As Colin Prescod has explained, much of the rhetoric displayed in the journal was a product of Ricky and Cecil's extensive political education and experience in Communist and Marxist organising spaces: 'Compared to me, they were really sophisticated. They were pretty well versed and educated in Marxist theory and activism. If you look at the *Liberator*, you can see it'.[57]

Gerlin's name appeared sporadically throughout *TBL*'s lifespan, listed among the members of its editorial committee. It seems that despite her involvement, she was not interested in contributing her own writing. Where mention of Black women and women-centred activism in *TBL* did appear, it was usually in conjunction with narratives on the significance of Claudia Jones to Britain's Black political landscape. The focus on Jones as a beacon for Black women's activism was likely inspired both by Ricky's experience of having worked with her before her passing and Colin Prescod's connection to her, as his mother and Claudia had worked closely together on anti-racist campaigns during the late 1950s and early 1960s. It's interesting that Gerlin did not utilise *TBL* to exercise her developing Black feminist consciousness. However, as we've established from Gerlin's move to the BLF and her deepening involvement with the young people of Brixton via the Gresham Project and Abeng Centre, Gerlin prioritised the principles of accessibility and inclusion, and also recognised how heavy political jargon could serve as an obstacle to meaningful engagement. She was conscious in avoiding language that could confuse more than it could inspire:

> I don't use certain language because I want people to understand, so we can't use these big, convoluted terminologies which no one really understands ... I always have a problem with the brothers, in the street or [when] I come to meetings, and they always use these words and I'm like 'who understands that?' ... My partner had a magazine ... Called *The Black Liberator* ... and the articles, they were good, they were dealing with many issues, but you couldn't understand it. I went and joined their collective and I said '... you need to change the language or otherwise, you're making this for university students ...' So they tried to do a bit of both to make it a bit easier in the later issues.[58]

Despite not writing for the journal, Gerlin was crucial to their production and providing a critical voice. Her home was used as both a meeting and production space for *TBL*. As Gerlin's daughter has attested, this sometimes proved detrimental to Gerlin and her family's private life, as the boundaries between her home as a living space and as community space were blurred. For Gerlin's daughter, this intrusion on her home space was sometimes uncomfortable.[59] Zainab Abbas also recalled the presence of *TBL* in Gerlin's home during her time staying there, remarking that the collective 'took over her kitchen'.[60] As well as Gerlin's home *TBL* also made use of her workspace, as Ricky used the Abeng Centre to distribute the journal and for correspondence from *TBL* subscribers and supporters. This encroachment upon Gerlin's physical spaces is brought into context when we consider that, for much of the 1970s, Gerlin and Ricky were in a relationship and lived together. In any case, this example of Gerlin's involvement in *TBL* and its presence in the life of her family shows the complications that her activism might have introduced to her personal life. There are also parallels that can be made between historical Black feminist figures and Gerlin in this instance, in the act of providing space for Black radical discourse and projects to take place. This is oftentimes an underrated contribution, but a necessary one for movements to develop and grow. For example, the Martiniquais, Paris-based sisters Paulette and Jeanne Nardal were catalytic figures in the Négritude movement, which developed in 1930s Paris. A form of cultural Pan-Africanism, the Négritude movement is often associated with male writers, thinkers and poets, namely those decribed as the 'Fathers of Négritude': Aimé Césaire, Léopold Senghor and Léon Damas. The work of the Nardal sisters remained overlooked until recently.[61] One of their major contributions to the movement, as well as theorisations, writing and publishing, was that the sisters opened up their apartments and salons as meeting places for Black intellectuals to socialise, exchange ideas and organise. In Britain, there is the example of Amy Ashwood Garvey, who opened the Florence Mills Social Parlour and the International Afro Restaurant during the 1930s, which served a similar purpose as a space for socialisation, political networking and shelter from racial discrimination and alienation in interwar London.[62] The cultivation and sharing of physical space is therefore an indelible contribution to Black political initiatives, oftentimes provided by Black feminist women.

One of the more directly interventionist activities of *TBL* that Gerlin participated in was its work in helping to establish the group Black People Against State Harassment (BASH). This project was convened in 1978 as a coalition between a number of Black and Asian activist groups. The context of BASH's founding was reported on by Colin Prescod in *TBL*: 'On Sunday 1 October 1978, eight militant Black organisations called a public meeting to start a campaign against state harassment of Black people'.[63] The impetus for the BASH initiative was the request by Metropolitan Police Commissioner David McNee to further extend police powers, and the prevalence of police brutality. The first meeting featured Cecil Gutzmore, Martha Osamor of the United Black Women's Action Group and the Scrap SUS campaign, Tariq Ali from Bradford Asian Youth, and Berry Edwards, a renowned Pan-African activist representing Manchester's West Indian Coordinating Centre. The Abeng Centre was used as the venue for this inaugural meeting, and alongside the aforementioned speakers, attending groups included: the Black Socialist Alliance, Mukhti (an Asian liberation collective), Brixton Ad-Hoc Committee against Police Repression, and the Brixton Black Women's Group.[64] As BASH gained traction it also attracted the participation of other groups such as Grassroots Bookstore, an offshoot project of the BLF, and the Black People's Information Centre, based on Portobello Road, Notting Hill.[65] As one of the representatives of *Grassroots*, activist Robert Singh recalled Gerlin and the Brixton Black Women's Group's active role in BASH, and the respect she had garnered by this time within the Black liberation movement:

> My interactions with Gerlin were during the time when BASH was in existence. A small number of Black Groups came together to campaign against the overbearing harassment of black communities by the state. The Brixton Black Women's Group, of which Gerlin was a key member, hosted meetings. I represented Grassroots Bookstore/The BLF at meetings. My memory of Gerlin is of a calm, articulate and passionate person who cared deeply of her community. She was well respected by those who attended the meetings.[66]

According to Robert, Gerlin and the BBWG did the majority of the practical work in BASH, and Gerlin especially handled the practical responsibilities such as setting up the group's accounts. Although, as Robert attests, there were some reservations and suspicions from men within BASH as well as the wider Black movement, that the BBWG were 'just a bunch of lesbians' due to their nature as an autonomous collective of Black women, their work within BASH and their other practical issues garnered them respect as a serious, political, and wide-ranging organisation.[67]

EMERGENCE OF THE WOMEN'S LIBERATION MOVEMENT

Simultaneous to the emergence of the Black Power movement, what became known as the 'second wave' women's liberation movement gained traction from the mid 1960s onwards. In this period the women's movement saw some significant gains, such as the Abortion Act of 1967, which legalised abortion on certain grounds, and the

Family Planning Act of the same year, which made the contraceptive pill more widely accessible via the NHS.[68] These advances in women's bodily autonomy and the widening of reproductive rights were among the most tangible advancements for women in the post-war period. But heightening conservative and right-wing backlash threatened to undo even slight improvements to women's rights. Wider access to abortion and birth control methods also failed to protect women and girls from experiencing discrimination and sexism in the healthcare system. In other areas such as the workplace, the private space of the home and in public, the power dynamics between women and men were wildly imbalanced, and there was not much evidence of improvement during the post-war period. Unequal rates of pay was another major issue in which little progress was made until the mid 1970s. The progress that was made was due in large part to industrial action undertaken by working-class women, such as in the case of the Ford and Grunwick strikes. In sum, by the 1970s patriarchal structures leading to gendered oppression persisted in many aspects of women's lives. The women's liberation movement had many issues to tackle on its agenda. But it also had internal difficulties to iron out.

Despite the important role working-class women played in advancing the rights of all women and people of marginalised gender identities, this was not reflected in the organised women's liberation movement in its early stages. The movement's instigators were mainly university educated, middle-class, white women.[69] One of the decisive events that helped to propel the movement forward was the first National Women's Liberation Conference, held in Ruskin College, Oxford, between 27 February and 1 March 1970. This event also held a mirror up to the discrepancies between the movement's initial leading activists and the wider population of women struggling for liberation. The event was organised by women who were students at Oxford, including feminist historian Sheila Rowbotham, and the initial idea was for the conference to take an historical focus. Importantly, the conference's reach extended far wider than fellow Oxford students or historians. It attracted over 600 women from across England, including Gerlin, and created the basis for an organised women's movement with regular conferences. It's not clear how Gerlin found out about the conference. It is also interesting that she attended the event by herself as opposed to as part of an organisational cohort, although she had no formal ties with women's groups at this time. It appears as if this was her first introduction to political organising under the auspices of women's liberation. In her *Shrew* interview a year after the conference, Gerlin stated that her inspiration to attend was born out of her unfamiliarity with feminist politics: 'I was interested, not knowing anything'.[70] This was representative of her approach to political movements during the early 1970s, when she principally sought to learn more and understand how to get involved. During the conference's proceedings, four official demands were agreed upon: equal pay; equal educational and job opportunities; free contraception and abortion on demand; and free twenty-four-hour nurseries.

Despite the importance of these demands, their scope was limited by comparison to demands made at future national conferences and those made independently by revolutionary organisations (though in 2023 they still have not all been met). For example, there was no inclusion of demands to end domestic abuse against women, and no mention of solidarity with women elsewhere in the world. Unlike the Black Power movement, the women's liberation movement in its early manifestation did not have an internationalist and anti-imperialist outlook. However, their first conference succeeded in creating a huge mobilising effect for the women's movement and inspiring the development of countless women's groups across Britain. It was a starting point, but as Gerlin and others recognised, there was much progress to be made in advancing the WLM's politics toward a more revolutionary direction. Perhaps the most obvious shortfall of this conference was the lack of acknowledgement of the issues and experiences of racialised women. This was Gerlin's takeaway from the experience; 'I couldn't pick up on the relevance as it pertains to Black women', she said of the conference.[71] For Gerlin, the absence of racialised women from the discourse in the event affirmed the need for a Black women's movement that was separate from the white and middle-class dominated mainstream women's liberation movement, of which the conference was representative. In her later interviews Gerlin used the event as a starting point for explaining why she went on to develop groups like the Brixton Black Women's Group. In Gerlin's recollection she arrived at the conference to find that she was one of only two Black women present. The other woman she encountered, Pat Smith, was a student at the University of Essex, and arrived with other students. Not only were there very few Black women present, but all the speakers were white. Feminist and anti-imperialist activist Diane Langford was a leading member of the Revolutionary Marxist Leninist League, which had links with liberation movements in Vietnam, Palestine, Southern Africa and elsewhere. She had invited one of her comrades from Zimbabwe, Eileen, to the conference in the hopes that she could convince the organisers to allow her to speak about the liberation struggles taking place in southern Africa: 'I'd persuaded her to accompany me imagining that, if she addressed the conference, the women gathered there would embrace the idea of international solidarity'.[72] Unfortunately, the organisers didn't take this offer up, and the conference featured no Black women speakers. Not only that, but Eileen was also subjected to racist harassment during the conference, when a white woman noticed her in the bathroom, grabbed her hair and commented that it looked like pubic hair.[73] It is perhaps not surprising that there were so few Black women attendees at the conference given that women's liberation was oftentimes viewed as a preoccupation of middle-class white women, and as a distraction from Black liberation.

The closest the conference got to addressing internationalism, anti-imperialism and matters of race, was a speech by Selma James. An intellectual and radical activist in her own right, James was also the wife of the Trinidadian Marxist historian C. L. R. James. According to Diane Langford, James spoke in a meeting in a side room, not as part of the plenary session.[74] Although as Gerlin attested to, the majority of the conference's discussions bore no relevance to the experiences of Black women or women of colour, Selma James brought with her an understanding of Black politics, anti-colonialism, anti-imperialism and anti-capitalist politics that caught Gerlin's attention:

She was the only one [who], when she spoke, made any connection to me. She's a Jewish woman but she's married to CLR James, the Trinidadian historian, and so she was coming from that experience of, you know, living with a black man, a black historian, so she could have that connection as she had information about the issues and kind of mentioned them in a particular way.[75]

For Gerlin, Selma James's perspective was an example of a broader view on women's liberation, one more closely linked to what we would now call intersectionality. This helped Gerlin to see how the politics of women's liberation could be aligned with the revolutionary politics of the Black Power movement and the anti-imperialist left. As the work of intersectional Black feminists has established, experiences of gendered discrimination and oppression are further complicated by race, class, sexuality, and other important facets of ourselves and of our communities' experience. This is something that had been acknowledged decades prior to the emergence of the women's movement by working-class Black women like Claudia Jones, who was writing about Black women's issues from a Marxist perspective as early as 1949. Gerlin further attested that Selma James 'put it all in context ... how it would affect black women and our involvement. Because our struggle wasn't just about women, it was an anti-imperialist struggle, about black *people*'.[76] Due to this experience, Gerlin was now sure of the compatibility of, and essential relationship between, women's issues and the broader issues facing Black people globally. From this point on Gerlin became more attentive to feminism. Certain that she would not benefit from participating in white-dominated women's groups, and with no alternative caucus for Black women yet established, she set to work creating one from within the Black Power movement, founding the BWAC and the BLF's women's caucuses.

Whilst helping to build up a Black feminist approach within the Black movement, it is clear that although Gerlin did not actively participate in the white, middle-class dominated wing of the women's liberation movement as a member of any such group, she at least had tangible links with them. *Shrew*, a product of the emergence of women's liberation politics in Britain, was a periodical which ran from the late 1960s into the late 1970s, and its production was a task that was rotated between different London-based women's liberation groups whose membership bases were self-proclaimed white and middle-class women. In the Summer

1978 issue of *Shrew*, for example, the writers openly admitted to their political limitations, stating: 'We are all white, and most of us are middle class in origin, ex college and in our mid/late twenties'.[77] In any case, Shrew performed an important duty in presenting discourse related to the project of women's liberation, and (to varying degrees) the need to oppose the white, patriarchal, capitalist system. Whilst issues of *Shrew* did occasionally make mention of race, and demonstrate at least an appreciation of anti-imperialism if not a consistent embrace of it. There is also no evidence to suggest Black women were ever involved in the magazine's production.[78] However, in the September 1971 issue, Gerlin was featured among three other women. She was the only Black woman among them. The aim of this issue was to present the experiences and perspectives of women the editing group deemed to be outsiders of the movement. Curiously, then, it seems Gerlin did not meet the criteria to be considered a participant of the movement for women's liberation. It's interesting to consider whether she was considered an outsider to the movement due to her Blackness, whether she was not identified as a participant because she was not attached to an official WLM group (although as we have explored above, she had by this time developed Black women's caucuses in pre-existent organisations), or if she herself was opposed to being described as a participant in the WLM:

> This issue of *Shrew* is made up of four interviews. This is how we chose to deal with the question: who are we in relation to other women not officially in the movement? It is a big question which we can only clarify, not answer.
>
> Those of us who worked on it learnt a lot about the question and therefore about ourselves: the struggle for the liberation of women is not confined to the women's movement. Rather the movement is an organised and, hopefully, a comprehensive expression of the daily lives and struggles of all women who in their millions make up the liberation struggle.[79]

Another intriguing aspect of this feature was that the *Shrew* writers described Gerlin as a 'middle class working wom[a]n', perhaps in recognition of her educational and family background, rather than her profession at the time of her interview, which was as a youth worker at the Seventies Coffee Bar.[80] As noted several times throughout this book, the outcome of this feature is the most candid interview recorded of Gerlin. It seems Gerlin felt safe or brave enough to delve into such personal questions with a women's liberation group. How the editing group located Gerlin for this feature is not mentioned, and so whether or not Gerlin was familiar with the group or the interviewer(s) is currently unknown.

GAY LIBERATION

Gerlin's 1971 feature in *Shrew* magazine was uncharacteristic in that it provided insight into the more personal details on her life, including her experience of falling pregnant and having her daughter, thoughts on marriage and relationships, her sexual identity and even how much money she spent each month. As her first interview this was perhaps a learning curve in terms of what she was and wasn't comfortable with making public, given how later she carefully avoided divulging personal information. In any case, as a researcher I am grateful that this interview exists as it is the only available evidence of Gerlin's participation in the movement for Gay Liberation. In this interview Gerlin refers to herself as bisexual and as a member of the Gay Liberation Front (GLF). How the GLF linked with Gerlin's other activist work and what drew her to becoming involved can be answered, at least in part, with a brief introduction to the GLF.

The movement for Gay Liberation was deeply intertwined with the Black Power movement, leftist and student movements, and the various countercultures of the late 1960s that bled into the next decade. While the Gay Rights movement had in earlier years involved campaigns for civil rights and social acceptance, the Gay Liberation movement was informed by the anti-imperialist left, the hippie movement and socialist politics. It called not for social acceptance but for a transformation of society and a total end to the oppression of marginalised groups. As articulated by co-founder of the GLF in Britain Aubrey Walters, 'it could easily see itself as part of the wider struggle for full human rights and liberation'.[81] The term 'gay' was at that time a catch-all term which was used to describe all non-heterosexual and trans people, much in the same way that 'queer' is used today. The Stonewall Riots of 1969 was a watershed moment, propelling a new generation of queer youth in a revolutionary direction. The Stonewall Inn was a queer bar in New York's Greenwich Village, which was subject to regular police harassment and raids, like most queer spaces at the time. One night in June 1969, the local queer community decided to physically fight back against state harassment after police attempted raided the building and shut it down. Crowds of angry young people, led by trans women and drag queens, managed to force police to retreat into the Inn and barricade themselves inside. This was a significant moment and spurred many queer young people to find ways to organise collectively with the aims of self-defence and community building.[82]

However, the evolution of the Gay Rights movement into the Gay *Liberation* movement was influenced by a myriad of events, including a speech by Huey Newton, the US Black Panther Party's co-founder and Minister of Defence (BPP) on 15 August 1970. This speech resulted in 'A Letter from Huey to the Revolutionary Brothers and Sisters About the Women's Liberation and Gay Liberation Movements', published in the *Black Panther* newspaper. The history of the BPP in the US has been attentively studied by scholars and subject to reflection by former leading members. While its formation, politics, survival programmes, wider influence on activist movements, and the role of women within the Party has received great interest, the BPP's history as it pertains to Gay Liberation has been woefully understudied.[83] Huey Newton's letter is a significant output that demonstrates the BPP's radical and inclusive vision for a positive future. It served as a clarification on the organisation's position on Gay and Women's Liberation, and encouraged Panther Party members both in the US to adopt a supportive position on both issues:

> During the past few years strong movements have developed among women and among homosexuals seeking their liberation. There has been some uncertainty about how to relate to these movements. Whatever your personal opinions and your

insecurities about homosexuality and the various liberation movements among homosexuals and women (and I speak of the homosexuals and women as oppressed groups), we should try to unite with them in a revolutionary fashion.[84]

This letter's influence was significant at the time, and remains a useful articulation of what solidarity between oppressed groups can look like. Newton called for an end to the view that homosexuality was an outcome of capitalist decadence as some believed it to be, stating that 'we should relate to the homosexual movement because it is a real thing'.[85] Huey Newton was wary of prejudices held by Party members, as a revolutionary force, which might result in the BPPP reproducing systems of oppression. The letter, which was met with some internal backlash – certainly by male members – led to teach-ins on the topic, in an effort to educate Party members on Gay Liberation and, if applicable, get them to confront their homophobia.[86] Despite the letter's positive step toward an intersectional framework, it implied that Gay Liberation was external to the BPP. Huey Newton failed to consider that there could be queer people among the BPP's own membership. At the same time, in Britain's Black Power movement the topic of Gay Liberation went largely undiscussed, even in the aftermath of this letter's publication. But as Black Power activists in Britain had access to copies of the *Black Panther* newspaper via radical bookshops who imported them from the US, they would have been aware of it. Regardless of the lack of response in the Black activist movement in the UK the letter quickly became famous, and Gerlin was likely familiar with it. One of the founders of Britain's GLF chapter, Aubrey Walter, attended the Revolutionary People's Constitutional Convention in Philadelphia, a meeting organised by the BPP to bring together different sections of the revolutionary movement and draft a new collective constitution. It considered gender identity as well as sexual orientation, settling on nineteen points for the final constitution that included:

- The right to be gay anytime, anyplace.
- The right of free physiological change and modification of sex.

- That a free education system present the entire range of human sexuality, without advocating any one form or style, that sex roles and sex-determined skills be not fostered by the schools.

- The abolition of nuclear family because it perpetuates the false categories of homosexuality and heterosexuality.

- The full participation of gays in the people's revolutionary army.[87]

Both the Revolutionary People's Constitutional Convention and its nineteen-point constitution are examples of how the Black Power Movement led the way for other radical liberation movements and encouraged unity between them. Like many young activists in this period, Aubrey Walter had spent time as a member of the Communist Party of Great Britain (CPBG). He then met with fellow Londoner Bob Mellors, who had spent time with the GLF's established New York chapter. After arriving back in London, they began setting up a chapter of the GLF there. Within its first few meetings, which were held in a lecture room at the London School of Economics, the GLF was regularly attracting hundreds of people, the majority of whom were arriving with prior activist experience. According to Lisa Powers, a former member and biographer of the GLF, the interests of people who were attracted to the GLF included: 'resistance to the Vietnam War, black rights, women's liberation, the underground press, the White Panthers (a support group to the Black Panthers), the International Marxist Group, the Communist Party, a wide variety of other leftist groups including Maoists, the drug culture, transsexuals and rent boys'.[88] The GLF was the most overtly political and radical organisation of the Gay Liberation movement. Given its radical position, as well as its connections with Black Power and other revolutionary traditions, it is not surprising that Gerlin gravitated toward the GLF. By the time of her *Shrew* interview in September 1971, she had become a part of its regular membership. When asked about her involvement in the GLF as a Black woman, Gerlin said:

I feel that as a person I should be free to do what I want to
do and proclaim my feelings. I can't say I joined GLF because
I don't think GLF has got a membership, but I go to GLF
meetings or GLF happenings, and I'm not embarrassed, or I
don't feel anything if someone I know sees me with a group
of homosexual people. But at the same time I don't make it
a point to say: 'I'm a homosexual', because I don't go around
saying 'I'm a heterosexual'. But if someone asks, then I say:
'Yes, I am a homosexual'. Well, bisexual, whatever-sexual.[89]

As explained by Gerlin above, whilst she didn't seek to hide her
sexual orientation and romantic relationships, she also didn't view it
necessary to proclaim them among people she knew. This perspective continued throughout her life, and also represents a wider
attitude of Black women activists in creating boundaries between
the 'personal' and the 'political' during the 1970s. As one of Gerlin's
longstanding comrades, Beverley Bryan recalls that Gerlin's own
perspective was the norm in collectives such as the Brixton Black
Women's Group (as we will see also in the following chapter):

What you felt about your personal relationships did not seem
important. I didn't know a lot about her personal life … I
didn't know until she wanted to share, even her relationships
with other women, and working with lesbian women. She was
quite open, she would talk, but it wouldn't be like the essential thing. She said that to me, 'you know, my personal life is
not the most important thing about the work we're doing'.
But, I knew she had relationships with other women.[90]

Gerlin's first relationship with a woman took place when she was
twenty-six. She noted that she was not involved in a gay social scene:
'The places where you met other gay people I would never have
gone to. So I would never have met anyone in that way'.[91] It's not
clear exactly how she met her partner, who she referred to publicly
only as 'M'. Although in this section we are mostly concerned with
how Gerlin's sexuality informed and influenced her activism and
political ideas, it's useful also to consider the dynamics of this relationship. From the below testimony, we can pick up that Gerlin

and 'M' were actively attempting to divest from a heteronormative relationship structure, and build a lasting, fluid connection that might take different forms at different times:

> I didn't have a homosexual relationship until I was twenty-six. I think I must have fancied women long ago but I never thought I would have a homosexual relationship until I met M ... It's nice, because we've been living together for about four years now and we're still not bored with each other and we always talk for hours. And at other times we can be silent and get on with our own thing. I think the reason for this is that we are totally independent of each other in most ways ... It's like an experiment: we've got all these ideas we're working out amongst ourselves, which are very difficult at times but we're trying to prove something, to see if it can work. We build up a relationship together, we're friends, we're very close friends mentally and physically. We think that we can expand from that because we think that two people just don't come together and then stop, that we've got more to give. That even if our sexual relationship finishes, and if either of us should go and live with somebody else, we'd still be friends. And that's what's lovely about it.[92]

Aside from Gerlin's mention of her involvement with the GLF in *Shrew*, it has been difficult to recover other evidence of her involvement with the group. Lisa Power, as biographer of the GLF, noted that among the Brixton-based GLF members she interviewed, no one recalled Gerlin being around, and that 'there were very few Black faces in GLF but some allyship in both Notting Hill and Brixton between movements'.[93] One former GLF member, Nettie Pollard, recalled seeing Gerlin at local meetings in Brixton: 'I do remember her presence and that she was an impressive speaker'.[94] However, it has been difficult to discern whether the meetings in question were organised by the GLF or otherwise, and what exactly the meetings were about. There was much crossover between sections of the revolutionary movement, the various countercultures in Brixton and indeed along Railton Road, which was known as the 'frontline'. For example, the South London Gay Community Centre was

based at 78 Railton Road from 1974, and out of it various gay liberation, self-help and community projects emerged.[95] Olive Morris
and Liz Obi's squatted flat was at 64 Railton Road, and the Sabaar
Bookshop run by the Brixton Black Women's Group was based at
121 Railton Road. Gerlin certainly would have crossed paths with
different Gay Liberation projects simply as a Brixton resident, and
it seems strange that other Brixton-based GLF members wouldn't
recall her involvement in the organisation given she was a well-
known figure in the area, unless she was only involved for a brief
time. It's also worth noting here that in 1971 Gerlin was not yet
residing in Brixton – she lived with 'M' in Tufnell Park. A year
later she moved to Brixton and began her relationship with Ricky
Cambridge. This goes some way to explain why Brixton-based
members of the GLF may not recall her involvement, since during
the time she was active in the organisation she was not yet well
known in Brixton, and after beginning her relationship with Ricky
it was not well known that she was bisexual (her testimony above
suggests she didn't commonly share this information). Although in
1971 she discussed her engagement in the GLF she never did again,
which suggests that her involvement may have been short-lived.
Her affiliation and involvement with the Black women's movement
was, as we will see, much more tangible, and has become what she
is most heavily associated with.

NOTES

1 Gerlin Bean, *Shrew*, 1971, p12.
2 Ansel Wong interviewed by the author, 15 April 2022, p1.
3 Rosie Wild, '"Black was the colour of our fight": Black Power in
   Britain, 1955-1976', University of Sheffield, 2007, p4. 2007, p4.
4 For more on the stylistic and cultural elements of Black Power, especially as it manifested in Brixton, see Tanisha C. Ford, *Liberated
   Threads: Black Women, Style, and the Global Politics of Soul*, University
   of North Carolina Press, 2019, pp123-210.
5 Robin Bunce and Paul Field, 'Obi B. Egbuna, C. L. R. James and the
   Birth of Black Power in Britain: Black Radicalism in Britain 1967–72',
   in *Twentieth Century British History*, Vol 22, No 3, 2011, pp391-414.
6 Stokely Carmichael, 'Toward Black Liberation', in *The Massachusetts
   Review*, Vol 7, No 4, Autumn 1966, pp639-651.

7   See Rob Waters, *Thinking Black: Britain, 1964-85*, University of California: California, 2019, pp1-4.

8   Ibid, p35.

9   Gerlin Bean, 'HomeBeats: Struggles for Racial Justice', CD Rom, Institute of Race Relations, 1998.

10 UCPA, 'Black Nurses Unite', Institute of Race Relations: 01/04/04/01/04/01/17.

11 Ibid.

12 UCPA, 'Announcement', *Black Power Newsletter*, Institute of Race Relations.

13 Ibid.

14 W. Chris Johnson, 'Guerrilla Ganja Gun Girls: Policing Black Revolutionaries from Notting Hill to Laventile', in *Gender & History*, Vol 26, No 3, 2014, p668.

15 UCPA, 'Black Power', Institute of Race Relations: 01/04/03/02/044.

16 Rosie Wild and Eveline Lubbers, 'Black Power – 3. Special Branch Files in context', specialbranchfiles.uk/special-branch-and-black-power, 17 September 2019.

17 Ibid, 'Black Power – 2. Main groups', specialbranchfiles.uk/2182-2/.

18 *Black Voice*, 'Long Term Programme'.

19 Gerlin Bean, 'The Heart of the Race: Oral Histories of the Black Women's Movement', 2009, Black Cultural Archives: ORAL/1/3, p5; heareafter BCA.

20 Ibid.

21 Alrick Cambridge, email correspondence with the author, 13 May 2021.

22 Denise Lynn, 'Socialist Feminism and Triple Oppression: Claudia Jones and African American Women in American Communism', *Journal for the Study of Radicalism*, Vol 8, No 2, Fall 2014, pp1-20.

23 Claudia Jones, 'An End to the Neglect of the Negro Woman!', in *Political Affairs*, National Women's Commission CPUSA: New York, 1949.

24 Bean 1971, op cit, p11.

25 Black Women's Action Committee, *Black Women Speak Out*, May 1971, p1; hereafter BWAC.

26 Ibid, p6.

27 Jo Robinson, 'Jo Robinson discusses Miss World contest', www.bl.uk/collection-items, 11 November 2011 - 4 December 2012.

28 Ibid.

29 BWAC, op cit, p1.

30 Ibid.

31 Ibid, p2.

32 Ibid, p3.

33 W. Chris Johnson, op cit, pp661-787.

34 National Conference on the Rights of Black People in Britain, 'National Programme for Action', Institute of Race Relations, p2.

35 Young Historians Project, 'We Are Our Own Liberators: The Black Liberation Front, 1971-1993', www.younghistoriansproject.org/black-liberationfront, October 2017.

36 'Editorial', *Grassroots*, Vol 1, No 1, 1971, p1.

37 Lester Lewis interviewed by Rosie Wild 2007, op cit, p94.

38 Zainab Abbas interviewed by the author and Hakim Adi, 15 April 2021, p5.

39 See W. Chris Johnson, '"The Spirit of Bandung" in 1970s Britain: The Black Liberation Front's Revolutionary Transnationalism', *Black British History: New Perspectives,* Zed Books, 2019, pp125-143. See also Anne-Marie Angelo, '"We all Became Black": Tony Soares, African American Internationalists and Anti-Imperialism', in Robin D. G. Kelley and Stephen Tuck (eds), *The Other Special Relationship: Race, Rights, and Riots in Britain and the United States*, Palgrave Macmillan: New York, 2015, pp95-102.

40 Bean 1971, op cit.

41 Beverley Bryan interviewed by the author, 7 March 2023; Gerlin Bean, 'Do you remember Olive Morris? Oral History Project', BCA: ORAL/1/8, p1; hereafter DYROM.

42 Bryan, op cit.

43 Ansel Wong interviewed by the author, 15 April 2022, p6.

44 Tony Soares interviewed by the author, 24 February 2018, p1.

45 Dada Imarogbe interviewed by the author, 29 December 2017.

46 Tony Soares, interviewed by the author, 24 February 2018, p3.

47 *Grassroots*, Vol 1, No 3, undated. George Padmore Institute: NEW/9/8; hereafter GPI.

48 Frances M. Beal, 'Black Women's Manifesto; Double Jeopardy: to be Black and Female', Third World Women's Alliance: New York, 1969.

49 *Grassroots* 1:3, op cit.

50 Gail Lewis interviewed by Rachel Cohen in 'Sisterhood and After: An Oral History of the Women's Liberation Movement', British Library: C1420/14, 2011.

51 Bean DYROM, op cit, p2.

52 *Grassroots*, Vol 1, No 4, undated. GPI: NEW/9/3.

53 Toni Morrison, 'What the Black Woman thinks about women's lib', *New York Times*, 22 August 1971.

54 Ibid.

55 This tagline can be found on the contents page of every issue of *The Black Liberator*.

56 Stella Dadzie interviewed by the author, 25 July 2019, p5.

57 Colin Prescod interviewed by the Young Historians Project, 15 September 2021.

58 Bean DYROM, op cit, p19.

59 Jennifer Hussey in conversation with the author, 27 May 2021.

60 Zainab Abbas in conversation with the author, 10 August 2022.

61 For more on the Nardal sisters and the Négritude movement, see Robert P. Smith, 'Black Like That: Paulette Nardal and the Negritude Salon', *CLA Journal*, Vol 45, No 1, September 2001, pp53-68; Emily Musil Church, 'In Search of Seven Sisters: A Biography of the Nardal Sisters of Martinique', *Callaloo*, Vol 36, No 2, Spring 2013, pp375-390.

62 For more information on Amy Ashwood Garvey in London, see Tony Martin, *Amy Ashwood Garvey: Pan-Africanist, Feminist and Mrs. Garvey No. 1 Or, a Tale of Two Amies*, The Majority Press, 2008; Marc Matera, *Black London: The Imperial Metropolis and Decolonization in the Twentieth Century*, University of California Press, 2015.

63 Colin Prescod, 'Black People Against State Harassment (BASH) campaign – a report', *The Black Liberator*, 1978.

64 Ibid.

65 Black People Against State Harassment (BASH) poster, c. 1979, Institute of Race Relations.

66 Robert Singh, email correspondence with the author, 29 March 2023.

67 Robert Singh in conversation with the author, 25 May 2023.

68 The grounds for termination of a pregnancy, as per the 1967 Act, were if a medical practitioner deemed the continuance of pregnancy to pose risk, greater than if the pregnancy were terminated, of injury to the physical or mental health of the pregnant woman. See British Pregnancy Advisory Service, 'Britain's abortion law', www.bpas.org/get-involved.

69 For more discussion on this, see Judith Orr, *Marxism and Women's Liberation*, Bookmarks: London, 2015.

70 Bean 1971, op cit, p11.

71 Bean 2009, op cit, p2.

72 Diane Langford, 'The Manchanda Connection: A Political Memoir', www.marxists.org.

73 Ibid.

74 Diane Langford interviewed by the author, 23 February 2022, p8.

75 Bean DYROM, op cit, p11.

76 Bean 2009, op cit, p3.

77 *Shrew*, Summer 1978.

78 Natalie Thomlinson, *Race, Ethnicity and the Women's Movement in England, 1968-1993*, Palgrave Macmillan, 2016, p46.

79 'Editorial', *Shrew*, Vol 3, No 8, September 1971, p1.

80 Ibid.

81 Aubrey Walter, *Come Together: Years of Gay Liberation*, Verso: London, 2018, p3.

82 See David Carter, *Stonewall: The Riots that Sparked the Gay Revolution*, St Martin's Press: New York, 2010.

83 Ronald K. Porter, 'A Rainbow in Black: The Gay Politics of the Black Panther Party', *Sexualities in Education: A Reader*, Peter Lang AG: New York, 2012, pp364-365.

84 Huey Newton, 'To the Revolutionary Brothers and Sisters', 15 August 1970, available at: https://issuu.com/randalljaykay/docs/aletterfromhuey.

85 Ibid.

86 Porter, op cit, p370.

87 Lisa Power, *No Bath but Plenty of Bubbles: An Oral History of the Gay Liberation Front, 1970-1973*, Continuum International Publishing Group, 1995, pp7-8.

88 Ibid, p16.

89 Bean 1971, op cit, pp11-12.

90 Bryan, op cit.

91 *Shrew*, 1971, p12.

92 Ibid.

93 Lisa Power, email correspondence with the author, 5 June 2022.

94 Nettie Pollard, email correspondence with the author, 31 July 2022.

95 Unfinished Histories, 'The South London Gay Community Centre', www.unfinishedhistories.com.

5

We had our own philosophy:
The Black women's movement

We had our own philosophy as Black women, we had our own
needs as Black women ... There were other women in other
organisations before us in Britain, but this was like the new
era, we were the new immigrants, so we started meeting.[1]

The Black women's movement is the part of Gerlin's activism
for which she is most celebrated. By this point Gerlin's capabilities as an organiser have been established: her ability to identify
a neglected site of struggle and illuminate it. In the last chapter we
explored Gerlin's initial efforts to organise women's caucuses within
two of the Black Power movement's foremost organisations, the
BUFP and BLF, to promote the concerns of women in the movement. We also surveyed her interactions with the white-dominated
women's liberation movement in 1970. With this in mind it
perhaps comes as no surprise that Gerlin continued along this path
of facilitation, helping pool together different Black women's caucuses who were already organising in mixed-gender groups, as well
as recruiting others on the margins of the Black movement to help
construct an autonomous Black women's movement. That movement developed its own philosophy built around Black women's
specific needs and concerns, all the while remaining interlinked
with the wider struggle for Black liberation. From the new understanding of women's issues in the Black Power movement of the
early 1970s, to the proliferation of Black women's groups
throughout Britain's major cities, and the emergence a Black

Women's Movement that matured into the 1980s, Gerlin was at the centre of these golden years. Throughout this time, Black women's groups sprang up around the country, in Liverpool, Leicester, Manchester, Birmingham, as well as the East London Black Women's Organisation (ELBWO), United Black Women's Action Group (UBWAG) and many others in London.[2] In 1978 the Organisation of Women of Asian and African Descent (OWAAD) emerged as an umbrella group to encourage the development of Black women's political organising, and the following year they convened the first National Black Women's Conference, attended by over 300 women. As we will see, Gerlin's contributions to this significant epoch were considerable. This chapter focuses on unfurling Gerlin's role as the 'mother' of the Black women's movement: as one of its leading facilitators, theorists, strategists and participants.

BRIXTON BLACK WOMEN'S GROUP - ORIGINS

Although neither the BLF nor the BUFP's women's caucuses appear to have been consistent or longstanding, they represent important milestones in the timeline of Black women's organising efforts. They also spurred on Gerlin and other women to build a more robust, long-lasting, and independent model that could help connect women from different branches of activism, and varying levels of organising experiences. This came to fruition in 1973 when the Brixton Black Women's Group (BBWG) was established, instigated by Gerlin. First-hand accounts regarding the creation of the BBWG vary, with BBWG activists holding differing perspectives on the circumstances of how the group was founded. According to Zainab Abbas, she and Gerlin of the BLF joined with Olive Morris and Liz Obi of the BPM, and another woman named Marcia who was not affiliated with a Black organisation, as the group's earliest members.[3] The women who came together to forge this group had varied reasons for doing so. The below testimony from Zainab gives an account of the group's very first meeting, and suggests Gerlin was the motivating force in the BBWG:

The Brixton Black Women's Group was set up because Gerlin said we should talk about issues relating just to Black women. And she got a group of us together. And we met at a sister's house, [who had] a small child ... Marcia... And we discussed issues related to feminism, defining feminism overall, and what it was about and then defining it in relation to black women, and then in relation to our own experiences, and it was good. It was a nice evening where we got together, then agreed to meet the following week because it was interesting enough for us to keep going with it. And we kept going and kept going. And then suddenly it got out about us.[4]

From Gerlin's perspective, the BBWG began as a marriage between activists of two of London's most active Black Power groups. As women from the BLF started to meet to discuss gendered issues, they joined with women from the BPM:

We didn't call it the Brixton Black Women's Group to start with, or the Black Women's Group, we started off just meeting as a collective, and we used to move around from different sisters' homes and have meetings in the evenings. I was in the Black Liberation [Front], Olive was in the Panthers, so they were separate groups with perhaps slightly different ideologies at the time. However, the women from the Panthers used to come and join with us as women, from the other group ... and then we would invite other women who weren't really aligned to anything to these meetings. Because at the time it was the men who were in control of everything, and they still are [laughter]. So we as women decided that we would meet together because we had issues as women separate from the national struggle, the Black struggle as a whole.[5]

Beverley's view of BBWG's emergence was informed by the fact that she was situated in the BPM, a mixed-gender group which had begun to disintegrate by 1973. For the Panther women keen to continue their work, the BBWG provided the opportunity to do so and expand the conversation around women's issues:

There were lots of tensions and issues that came up, especially among the men in authority quarrelling over their positioning, and after about three years that particular organisation started to fall apart. But a number of the women who were involved in it and a couple of the more conscious men, felt that they didn't want the work that was being done to simply stop.[6]

The BBWG, in its embryonic stage, did not keep records such as meeting minutes that might provide information on the nature of its formation. As a result, the story has to be pieced together through the subjective recollections of those who were involved, which naturally vary between members. Other members of BBWG, who, although not present during the time of its formation, picked up fragments of information pertaining to this time, include Gail Lewis, who joined the BBWG several years into its existence:

When I joined Brixton Black Women's Group, it had been in existence for several years, but it started as a reading group in the Sabaar Bookshop. I think it was women who were involved in *Race Today* who started it.[7]

One conclusion we can draw from the varying recollections of BBWG's founding is that the women who were integral to the group's formation did not intentionally set out to build a structured and influential organisation that would go on to serve as the vanguard of the Black women's movement in Britain. Rather, the BBWG began as a series of gradual steps by women, informed by their experiences of the Black Power movement and revolutionary activism, to carve out a distinctive space to explore the gendered dimensions of their struggles as working-class Black women, and members of a wider global anti-imperialist, anti-capitalist struggle. BBWG's development into a fully-fledged political force was organic, and thus the founding women were not concerned with the task of documenting this historic moment. For Beverley and other Panther women, the BBWG offered an opportunity to continue the organising work that was no longer being done by the BPM. Perhaps the prospect of a women's-centred organising environment was also appealing in that it reduced the possibility of arguments

related to status and positioning. Beverley, Olive and Liz all gravitated to the BBWG when the BPM ceased activity, while both
Zainab and Gerlin continued participation in the BLF, which was
still active. Alongside BPM and BLF activists, the BBWG was also
joined by women from the *Race Today* collective, which was founded
by Darcus Howe in late 1973. Leila Hassan Howe, for instance,
was involved with BBWG for a short while. Due to the diverging
politics of these different groups, and the individual opinions of
the women involved, there were several topics which were viewed
with varying degrees of relevance and importance. The earliest
point of contention was 'Wages for Housework', a campaign which
emerged initially from the Italian women's movement in 1972, and
which argued for the redistribution of wealth produced by unpaid
domestic workers and housewives to combat the economic subjugation they experienced. The basis of the disagreement within BBWG
pertained to the campaign's perceived relevance to working-class
Black women in Britain. Selma James, who featured in the previous
chapter as a speaker at the first Women's Liberation conference,
and who was married to Trinidadian historian C. L. R. James, was
involved in the Black movement and had a level of influence on the
organisations and collectives in which he participated. As Darcus
Howe's uncle and political mentor, C. L. R. James, the Caribbean's
foremost Marxist and Trotskyist thinker of his generation steered
the ideological direction of the *Race Today* collective, to the extent
that it has been described as 'Jamesian' in nature.[8] In March 1972, at
the third National Women's Liberation conference in Manchester,
Selma James delivered a talk in favour of Wages for Housework,
and was met largely with criticism by attendees. At the conference,
she explained later, women were critical of the idea that women
should not seek paid employment outside of the household instead
of campaigning for wages for housework: 'most of the women at
the conference where I put it forward, were very hostile to the idea
that women should not necessarily go out to work, because they felt
(that's how) women's consciousness would be raised'.[9]

In the aftermath of the conference Selma James wrote a pamphlet
entitled 'Women, the Unions and Work, Or... What is Not to Be
Done'. Although written by her it was published by the Notting
Hill Women's Liberation Workshop Group, and therefore reflected

this group's collective views. Reading its contents with the knowledge that the campaign had been met with criticism not long before provides a substantial aid in dissecting its argument. Much of the contents can be viewed as a response to the criticisms James heard at the conference in Manchester:

> The demands at the end of the paper aroused most interest at the conference. And were discussed, added to and modified there. But there may have been some misunderstanding about their purpose. They are not a statement of what we want, finally, to have. They are not a plan for an ideal society. And a society based on them would not cease to be oppressive. Ultimately the only demand which is not co-optable is the armed population demanding the end of capitalism.[10]

The title of the pamphlet, a nod to Lenin's famous work of 1901 *What Is To Be Done*, indicates Selma James's Marxist schooling, and the rhetoric throughout provides assurance that she maintained her revolutionary position in theorising women's liberation. In sum, for Selma James and fellow supporters of the campaign, Wages for Housework was an opportunity to 'mobilise women, both "inside" and "outside" the women's liberation movement'.[11] While the women from *Race Today* collective argued for the relevance of Wages for Housework to the struggles of Black women, others thought that it was a preoccupation of bourgeois sections of the women's movement. Zainab recalled being one of the strongest critics of the campaign in the BBWG: 'They were asking us to discuss this uber middle class concept of wages for housework. It was just so far out of our experience that it just didn't relate to me at all. So I reacted very strongly against it'.[12] The BBWG maintained this position against Wages for Housework, and other perceived bourgeois trends in the WLM, into its later years, stating in 1977: 'Although the women's movement has highlighted many important issues, we do not subscribe to that tendency within it which regard men as the primary source of oppression and which sees women's liberation solely in terms of sexual emancipation, neither do we support the call for wages for housework'.[13] This split between the women from *Race Today* and other members of the Brixton group is cryptically referred to in a later oral history interview with Gerlin: 'The *Race Today* women, they decided that they wouldn't come with the Brixton Black Women's Group. So we separated at that point, there was a split. There have always been splits in the black movement'.[14] Although she didn't divulge the circumstances of this particular split, this comment from Gerlin seems to attribute it to the usual phenomenon of ideological differences within political movements. In the Black Women's Movement, even in its embryonic form, women hashed out various theories and ideas in small group settings, which, as we will see, gradually became bigger and more organised projects.

As the BBWG developed over the years, it naturally grew a larger membership. One of the ways it did this was by established members inviting other women, especially those on the margins of political activity, into the fold. Gerlin was adept at taking others under her wing, and this was most evident in the testimonies of women she recruited into the BBWG. One of these women was Melba Wilson. Originally from Texas, she arrived to London in 1977 having relocated with her British husband. For Melba, who was adjusting to life in England, the BBWG offered a pathway to becoming more rooted in the Black community in Britain, and Gerlin was instrumental in this process:

> Through Gerlin, it was like finding a lifesaver, because Gerlin invited me to join the group. It was for me, I describe it as a lifesaver, because I had come from living in the United States in a predominantly black milieu. And having come to London, and not knowing any black people in the UK, I was desperate to find communities of colour.[15]

Gail Lewis, born in Walthamstow in 1951, was just nineteen years old when she first met Gerlin at a meeting hosted by the West Indian Student's Centre in Earls Court. The event speaker was Penny Jackson, sister of George Jackson, one of the Soledad Brothers. George Jackson, incarcerated as a young Black man in the US, became an influential Black revolutionary thinker while in prison, delivering his condemnation of racism in a famed publication *Soledad Brother*, a collection of his prison letters, in March 1971. Penny Jackson was in the UK as part of a tour to raise support for her brother's defence

campaign. Inspired by the publication Gail attended the meeting and
met Gerlin, who had organised the event. After tentatively entering
into the Black liberation movement with Gerlin's guidance, Gail
became somewhat estranged from it due to other life circumstances,
until she returned several years into the BBWG's existence:

> I met Gerlin there and she took me to some other meetings
> and I was involved for a while, but I was also young and I was
> living out in Harrow, and I just lost connections with that.
> Then when I went back, when I went to university at LSE
> she was just finishing a degree there and we met and then she
> brought me to Brixton Black Women's Group and from that
> we started to work together much more and Brixton Black
> Women's Group got bigger and bigger.[16]

Gerlin's sphere of influence during her time in BBWG extended
beyond the group to include members of the predominantly white
WLM. Between 27 and 29 June 1975, the Polytechnic of Central
London, now the University of Westminster, hosted a conference
entitled 'Politics and the Women's Movement'. On 28 June Gerlin
led a session alongside Althea Jones-Lecointe titled 'Black women
in Britain'.[17] One of the attendees was Sheila Rowbotham, one of
the main organisers of the National Women's Liberation conferences since its inception in 1970, and a leading figure in Britain's
WLM. Sheila later recalled the event in her memoir: 'Both had
straddled divides of race and gender, as well as men in the black
movement who sidelined women's issues'.[18]

The BBWG was, at the point of its establishment in 1973, the
only autonomous Black women's group in London. Unbeknownst
to the women of the BBWG at the time, Liverpool Black Sisters had
emerged in the same year.[19] Then, in 1974, the Manchester Black
Women's Cooperative was formed by seasoned activists who, similarly to the BBWG, had acquired years of experience in the Black
Power movement.[20] The Manchester group was largely driven
by Ada Phillips, the wife of former UCPA activist Ron Phillips,
and sister of Kath Locke and Coca Clarke, also former members
of Manchester's UCPA branch and subsequently the BUFP.[21]
Although the motivations and concerns of these Black women's

groups all correlated, they were not immediately aware of each other's existence. It was for this reason that the BBWG initially referred to itself as the 'Black Women's Group', on the assumption that they were the only group of its kind and thus there was no need to use a location-specific name.[22] It didn't take long for them to forge connections with other women's groups, and prior to the late 1970s the Black women's groups in existence reflected similar political outlooks. As the first such group in London, and one of the earliest to form nationally, the BBWG had the task of carving out a philosophy and programme of activities, as stated by an anonymous BBWG member in 1985: 'There were no models for us to follow, no paths laid out. We just had to work it out as we went along'.[23] Prior to BBWG's major projects, such as its newspaper *Speak Out* and its work in setting up the Brixton Black Women's Centre, the BBWG worked on hashing out its collective ideology via study groups and discussions. With the majority of founding members having arrived in the group via the Black Power movement, there was already a firm basis of understanding around revolutionary traditions. The difference now was that women were organising in an atmosphere many found more supportive and productive, being devoid of male chauvinistic tendencies, which allowed them to prioritise the gendered dimensions to Black liberation. There are numerous statements on the difficulties some women found in working in mixed-gender organisations, mostly relating to the relegation of women members to the more domestic duties of taking meeting minutes and even making the tea.[24] There were also the social implications of young men and women working alongside each other; as the authors of *Heart of the Race* explained: 'We could not realise our full organisational potential in a situation where we were constantly regarded as sexual prey'.[25] Without these hindrances, Black women could set the political agenda on their own terms.

DEVELOPING A BLACK FEMINIST PHILOSOPHY: A GUIDE TO ACTION

Due to its origins in the Black Power movement, there was a clear Marxist-Leninist lineage to groups such as the BUFP, the BPM and the BBWG. The political writings of Marx and Engels, Mao Tse Tung and other similar works were considered required reading for radical Black activists. Accordingly, Black Power groups hosted study sessions to break down the theories presented by these works. The BBWG also served this purpose as a highly politicised study group, with the additional aim of relating the theories they were digesting to the conditions faced by Black women in their main sites of struggle. As Beverley Bryan recalled:

> It started off as a much more Marxist-Leninist women's group. We were that kind of women's group. The first thing we read was *The Communist Manifesto*. And one of the other things we read was Engels, *The Origins of the Family, Private Property and the State*. I think that gives you an indication of the early years, of just how much of a Marxist group that was. It was trying to show the origins of patriarchy but clearly linking it to capitalism. That's really important, I always remember those ideas coming to us out of that kind of study. So you can say our idea was that certain things were political. The culture wasn't seen as so important, it really was the way in which capitalism organises, and in some ways destroys relationships.[26]

This set-up as a study group seems to have been the first manifestation of the BBWG, before they began to plan a wider range of initiatives. The BBWG's study sessions worked to raise the political consciousness of the group as a whole, and through this determine the way forward in tackling their concerns. As more women began to attend from different sections of the Black movement, the potential influences of the group widened. This process was later explained by Gerlin:

> We met mostly as a study group to start with, to be informed, to raise our consciousness, to know what it was that we wanted to organise about but at the same time not forgetting the wider struggle. We were coming from all different perspectives, because you had so many organisations. You had cultural nationalists, you had socialists, you had Maoists, you

had Marxist/Leninists – you had all the -ists and the -isms and it was a melting pot of all sorts of things. I don't know if it was confusion, but I think it was a good time.

Another source of influence, as Zainab recalled, was Gerlin's earlier exposure to feminist politics due to her attendance at the first National Women's Liberation Conference in 1970, as well as the fact that she was around ten years older than most of the other activists she worked alongside:

> There's no doubt, that ten-year, eleven-year age gap between her and us meant that she was much more conscious on feminism, and the issues surrounding black women. So she could lead debates and stuff … While we were defining what feminism was, this is where Gerlin's lead mattered, because she was very much part of the whole feminist structure beforehand.[27]

Later, the BBWG came to explicitly define itself as a Black socialist feminist project. Women from both Black women's groups and white Leftist groups were wary of tendencies in the WLM that sought to blur 'personal life and feelings' with the 'political'.[28] At times this viewpoint was challenged by some BBWG members; Melba Wilson argued for the need to include consciousness raising practices within the group's programme, but the majority viewed it as a distraction from more pertinent issues. This is a topic that former BBWG members still grapple with in hindsight. Melba, as one of the strongest voices for consciousness raising, has since laid out why it was not deemed viable at the time:

> There was so much to do. In terms of it, really, we needed a political group. We needed to come up with a political statement of who we were. I can see the argument that would say, it would dilute things and the energies. Because it required a lot of energy just birthing this political group and sustaining it. So probably, it might have been that we didn't have enough energy or enough people, because really, there weren't that many of us. There were only about a dozen or so people. And we all had day jobs, or were studying. So could have

diluted the energies doing more personal stuff. And also, I
didn't want just a consciousness raising group. But I think at
some point we had set out our stall as Black socialist feminist.
It could have enhanced the group to be to be able to bring
some of the other stuff that was below the surface in terms
of our individual heritages or our family situation, or our
understanding of who we were as women and Black women
as opposed to Black political women. So, yeah, I think it
would have been enhanced, but it would have required even
more effort on our energy. And as I said, that was hard, those
years were very full on.[29]

Interestingly, other members who were averse to the idea of incor-
porating consciousness raising into the BBWG at the time have
since come to appreciate its value, as demonstrated by Gail Lewis
here:

Others, and I was in the others of us at the time, were saying,
'No, this in the end will individualise too much'. I don't think
that now. I think it depends what we're doing, what it's in
the service of. So I think I have a more complicated understanding now. But at the time, there was a divide, when you
know Black people were dying, Black women were working
two, three, four jobs, struggling to keep the kids together.
Our focus on the raising of consciousness around structural
issues felt more important. More urgent, there was an urgency
perhaps.[30]

These conversations about consciousness raising around personal
issues and identity, reveal the highly politicised state of the BBWG,
and the group's ambitions for building a strong foundation, using
Black socialist feminism as its pillars. They also found that their
stance on this issue set them apart from other manifestations of
Black women's organising in other areas of the Black Atlantic. In
the aftermath of Olive Morris's passing from leukaemia at the age
of twenty-seven, Gerlin and Stella Dadzie took a trip together to
America. They connected with Black women's groups there, and
Stella recalled one interaction with a Black women's group during

their stay in the Southside of Chicago, where the different priorities between the movement in Britain and the US took them by
surprise:

> We hooked up with a Black women's group there and attended
> a couple of their meetings, and we were very bemused because
> we'd looked at America as a leading voice, and we realised
> when we started engaging with these sisters, we were far more
> radical and far more grounded in the class politics ... We
> went to a meeting, where they wanted to discuss the colour
> of their nipples, and don't forget in them days we were still
> reclaiming blackness, we were still reclaiming the notion
> that black women could be beautiful, so they were necessary
> discussions, I guess, within that context and within that time,
> but so very different to the things that we were talking about
> here – police brutality, SUS laws. [31]

As a co-founding member and central organiser of the BBWG,
the degree to which Gerlin's own political philosophy flowered
throughout the early 1970s, and therein helped to shape the
direction of the BBWG, is easily identifiable. Stella described
Gerlin's political style, and the influence it had on her as their
bond strengthened during their US trip: 'Looking back I probably
learned a lot from Gerlin. She had a very pragmatic, down to earth
way of looking at the world. She and I went around America one
summer together, so we got to know each other really well. I'd
always looked at her and thought, "She's a serious woman, I should
listen to her. What she says makes sense"'.[32] The group asserted that
class struggle was essential to, and intertwined with, women's liberation. They also emphasised the added dimension of race, and drew
on historical examples of Black struggle, maintaining that women
had always been on the frontlines, from leading slave rebellions in
the Caribbean and the Americas to the contemporary struggles for
liberation against colonialism in Africa, and the fight against state
racism in the West. Despite accusations by some men that autonomous Black women's projects would sow divisions in the Black
movement, the BBWG were clear from the outset that they were
staunchly committed to Black liberation:[33] 'We the Black Women's

Group do not see ourselves isolated from the wider society and are joint in our efforts with Black men to triumph over racism in every form … Our ideological standpoint will not allow us to concentrate merely on sexual discrimination though we are bound to recognise it'.[34] The BBWG distilled the unique position of the Black woman as 'race, class and sex oppression under capitalism'.[35] Having arrived at a self-definition, the BBWG maintained a consistent politics throughout its lifespan.

BBWG INITIATIVES

The BBWG held meetings every Sunday from 3–5 p.m. They set about producing an organisational newsletter, *Speak Out*, where they could espouse their political focus and provide contributions to revolutionary discourse. The first issue of *Speak Out* was undated, but was likely produced around 1977.[36] It featured a comic strip illustration with four panels highlighting the struggles Black women had been involved in since the dawn of capitalism. The first panel featured a map of the 'triangular trade', highlighting the Slave Trade's theft of human life for profits, which funded the Industrial Revolution. The second panel featured a drawing of Harriet Tubman armed with a gun, in the process of liberating an enslaved man. The third panel illustrated Black women's role in production, showing two women at work in a factory setting. The fourth and final panel, set in Africa, showed women guerrilla fighters holding guns, with a baby wrapped on one of the women's back. The comic strip, though uncredited, was a clear proclamation of the BBWG's philosophy. The pages of *Speak Out* also provide us with a useful indication of the kind of topics which were high on the BBWG's agenda; these ranged from health (such as awareness-raising articles on sickle cell anaemia, which predominantly affects Black communities), and reproductive issues (concerns around birth control methods such as the Depo-Provera and Norethisterone injections), Third World politics, challenges to various forms of state racism, book reviews and poetry. In this way, the contents of *Speak Out* was like most other Black organisational newspapers of the time. It was also similar in that the articles were all uncredited, in line with the group's non-hierarchical approach.[37] Over the years, the topics in *Speak Out* steadily transitioned to reflect the wider political shifts taking place in the Black liberation movement between the late 1970s and early 1980s. Its earlier issues largely focused on issues pertaining to Britain's Black community and its radical rhetoric corresponded with that of its Marxist-Leninist and Black Power influences. The pages were filled with mentions of some of the major campaigns of the Black movement in which BBWG was involved, such as 'Scrap SUS' (which was largely led by women, including Mavis Best, and the women of the United Black Women's Action Group) and Black People Against State Harassment (BASH).[38] From the 1980s onwards, *Speak Out* responded to the worsening economic conditions in Britain, as the Thatcherite government announced devastating cuts to the public sector. In this decade, *Speak Out* also began to feature a greater number of initiatives from the women's liberation movement, and showcased BBWG's collaborations with feminist projects. For example, *Speak Out* featured advertisements for *Outwrite*, an 'internationalist feminist' newspaper founded in 1982 in East London, run by both Black and white women. *Outwrite*'s emphasis on liberation struggles in El Salvador, Palestine, South Africa and elsewhere, as well as women-led campaigns in Britain, made it politically compatible with BBWG.[39] Despite this compatibility, it is doubtful that the BBWG would have been so comfortable in promoting multiracial coalitions in its earlier years, and this is reinforced by a read through earlier issues of *Speak Out*. In addition to this, *Speak Out* also documented the casualties suffered by the Black women's movement, such as the untimely passing of activists Olive Morris (in 1979) and Sylvia Erike (in 1983).[40]

Alongside *Speak Out*, another key aspect of the BBWG's remit was running the Sabaar bookshop on 121 Railton Road in Brixton. This space was squatted by Olive Morris and Liz Obi, who lived in the upstairs flat before eventually moving to 64 Railton Road. For a time they were also joined by Zainab Abbas.[41] Sabaar, which was likely the first Black bookshop in Brixton, specialised in resources on Third World politics, alongside other topics such as education, political theory, women's liberation and children's books. The Sabaar bookshop was just one of the BBWG's practical, community-oriented initiatives, and it existed as part of the wider radical and Black independent bookshop movement.[42] Sabaar was also a reaction to the educational racism experienced by Black children in schooling, as demonstrated by the material it stocked. Beverley recalled the BBWG producing a book as part of efforts to promote cultural pride, interest in Black histories, as well as academic achievement for Black children. The BBWG reported via *Speak Out* that 'through the Sabaar Bookshop Collective we are able to keep in contact with schools and other institutions with whom we discuss educational material available in the bookshop for their use'.[43] In addition, Sabaar also demonstrated the BBWG's sustained involvement in the Black movement. It was a collaborative project between activist men and women alike, with a rota system that shared volunteer responsibilities between BBWG and mixed-gender groups, as BBWG member Jocelyn Wolfe attested, 'because that was a community project that we did together'.[44] However, though Sabaar began as a community-oriented, volunteer-run project, contentions arose over the question of utilising state funding to stabilise the project. As Gerlin recalled, the BBWG eventually applied for Urban Aid funding via the Section 11 Local Governments Act. Established in 1968, the aim of the Urban Aid programme was to fund projects in areas experiencing 'severe social deprivation'. In particular, projects which pertained to education, childcare, and welfare services for marginalised communities were applicable.[45] As it turned out, state-funding would gradually unravel the important work of the BBWG over the years in constructing the bookshop as a political initiative underpinned by the group's own revolutionary ideals. From Gerlin's recollections, one of the major voices against applying for funds was Olive Morris, who pointed out this contradiction:

Several of us, we ran it ourselves without any money … I was at university so I had a lot of free time and we used to just keep it open. When urban aid – they were offering money for development projects, in Lambeth, we applied under that scheme and Olive Morris – up until today, I respect her – because she said, 'You guys, don't go for that money because of the restrictions', and she was so correct, in the end. They will destroy it because they'll want to control it.[46]

Much has been written about the Section 11 scheme and its 'pacifying' effect on Black community initiatives.[47] For example, between the years of 1981 and 1982, 20 per cent of available funds were given to Black organisations, and this rose to over 50 per cent by 1986.[48] Given that the government rhetoric under Thatcher was that Britain was 'swamped' by immigrants, it might seem counterintuitive that what would have been considered radical projects were chosen for funding. However, as the experience of the Sabaar bookshop and other projects demonstrates, there is basis to conclude that this was part of a widespread effort to co-opt such organisations.[49] There were differing perspectives within the Black women's movement on how state funding might be viewed. For some, it was long-overdue compensation for the history of subjugation, exploitation and harassment of Black communities. As the East London Black Women's Organisation saw it, there was no contradiction in using state funds to develop their organisation since they believed the money rightfully belonged to them as a form of reparative justice,[50] whereas the Abasindi Co-operative in Manchester was vehemently opposed to external funding and opted to rely on their own skillsets to raise funds for their activities, which included making and selling their own clothes and hair plaiting.[51] For the BBWG, however, Section 11 funding changed the dynamic of the Sabaar project. With stable finances the group were able to recruit employees, which removed the onus on BBWG members and other local Black activists to contribute their time on a volunteer basis. This was not without some compromise on the group's value system. As Sabaar was now monitored by employees, it proved difficult to ensure the same political principles which underpinned the bookshop were upheld. In addition to this, at the turn of the 1980s Gerlin and other women in the BBWG began to seek out other terrains. Gerlin left for Zimbabwe in 1983, and thus ceased her direct activity with both the BBWG and Sabaar. The departure of longstanding members such as Gerlin, and the ideological disparities between them and the younger people who were becoming involved, left a vacuum.

Somebody like myself – I left at a probably crucial time. I went off to Zimbabwe, Beverley Bryan went someplace. And

so new people [were] coming in not having the same philosophy about the books, what you sell, why you are selling
them. Why we go on the outside – we didn't just [get people
to] come into the bookshop. Every morning we used to set up
outside so that the people passing by or people not reading,
we would have a discussion with you about what we were
doing. I think it lost some of those and then it broke down.[52]

Another practical initiative by the BBWG was the Black Women's
Centre at 41 Stockwell Green, Brixton. Opened in 1980, the Centre
was a collaboration between the BBWG and the Mary Seacole
Craft Group.[53] The Mary Seacole Group emerged out of a conversation at a BBWG meeting in 1976, wherein a member suggested
that mothers, and in particular single mothers, were suffering
from isolation, confined to the home and therefore disconnected
from community life. The Mary Seacole group was established
in October of that year and 'aimed at bringing together unsup-
ported mothers, both Black and white, and particularly the young
and inexperienced'.[54] As Marlene Bogle, member of the BBWG
reported, this initiative enabled several of the women to return
to college and some to part-time work'.[55] This development also
led the BBWG to conclude that, with an expansive programme of
activities, the group had matured to the point of requiring a perma-
nent physical home, 'where we could continue to develop our ideas
and provide facilities for women and children to meet on a regular
basis'.[56] The BBWG began work to obtain funding in July 1979,
and by September 1980 the Black Women's Centre was opened to
the community.[57] It provided numerous services, along the lines of
practical welfare support, childcare, political education and crafts.
As Gerlin explained, the Centre served as a respite for local women,
as a place to gather and receive community care, political nourish-
ment and contribute to the BBWG's activities:

We had a Black women's centre in Brixton. That was to
provide a safe space for women to come in and to reason with
other women and to develop themselves – just to read a book,
or get away, and we provided a crèche – so we had nice safe
spaces.[58]

The Centre's facilities quickly grew to include a reference library, art and craft workshop, and an information and advice service specialising in issues such as housing, education, legal advice, social security and welfare benefits.[59] As Gerlin attested to, the Centre was also utilised as a community meeting space, and became a key venue for Black activists, both women and men, to come together, discuss important issues, and strategise:

> We were supportive of the brothers and they did come to the centre for meetings – we allowed them to come in. We had open days when they could all come in and share.[60]

THE ORGANISATION OF WOMEN OF ASIAN AND AFRICAN DESCENT

The BBWG, and Gerlin as a key member, aided in the advancement of the Black women's movement as a coordinated, ever-expanding and determined political programme. Alongside other Black women's collectives that had emerged in the early 1970s, the BBWG had helped to sow the seeds for autonomous Black women's organising, and by the late 1970s the movement required a national body to continue this positive development and aid in encouraging other women to take up the task of organising. What was initially called the Organisation of Women of Africa and African Descent was formed in February 1978, not to replicate the work of existing women's groups, but to provide a national network for these groups to support each other's work and collaborate on projects. As its initial name suggests, it was also set up with a Pan-Africanist lens, and Black women in Britain took the lead from African women who were active in the African Student's Union (ASU), many of whom were involved in liberation organisations, and some of whom were active fighters in liberation wars in their homelands. Founding members included Gerlin, Beverley Bryan, Gail Lewis and Stella Dadzie, as well as African students from Ghana, Eritrea and Ethiopia. These origins were summarised by the BBWG five years later:

It was not the first or the only Black women's organisation. In other areas, African women, such as ZANU women's league were forming separate caucuses to their national liberation organisations. Black women resident or born in England were beginning to meet in study groups; still others had begun self-help groups like the Manchester Black Women's Co-op; others were spearheading the 'Stop SUS' campaigns. OWAAD performed a different function. It presented as a possibility, a chance for Black women all over England, to meet with each other, share ideas and give help and support to what each were doing.[61]

Not long after its establishment, the Organisation of Women of Africa and African Descent responded to calls from Asian women that they too should be included. The women on the organisation's central committee agreed that, due to the similarities between the experiences of African, Afro-Caribbean and Asian women in Britain, the organisation should involve all such women. This culminated in the subtle name change to: the Organisation of Women of Asian and African Descent (OWAAD). After this reorientation, the next substantial task for the organisation was to facilitate the first National Black Women's conference, which was convened on 18 March 1979 at the Abeng Centre. Gerlin recalled that the conference organising was conducted by about six people, and there was no way they could have predicted its success: 'It was about six of us who planned and organised it. We were panicking because we didn't know that people would come'.[62] Three decades later during an interview, Gerlin could still recall her emotions on the day, largely her nervousness upon realising how many women had travelled to the conference: 'We couldn't believe it … I used to smoke cigarettes a lot, and I was like a chain smoker and I was chairing the meeting – we were all nervous'.[63] In fact, somewhere between 250-300 women responded to the conference's advertisement – a testament to the great political appetite of Black and Asian women in Britain at this time – eager to forge connections with each other and participate in the discussions. Women arrived from all across England. The recollections of attendees all point to the conference's electric atmosphere.[64] Video footage of the event documented this energy, a palpable excitement permeates the moving image.[65] For many of the women attending it was a transformational experience that showcased how women could be at the forefront of radical events, as leading organisers, chairs and speakers, raising issues affecting Black and Asian communities, as well as those specific to women. Ama Gueye's summary of that first conference encapsulates its powerful impact on the women present:

It was the first time up to that point in this country, anyway in my adult life, that I saw women talking on a platform, up until then there'd only been men who had been keynote speakers ... I didn't know that we could be on a platform and say these things ... And from the get-go, they were saying 'Right, you've seen how we can organise, we can all come together and give each other strength, unity is strength. The things that are going on in your communities, whether it's to do with education, health, immigration, employment, all these things which we were being discriminated against, we can organise it. You can go do it in your own communities'. And we were fired, I tell you, I think from that first day we were at the OWAAD conference, most of us walked on air [laughter], I don't know for how many months afterwards. And sisters all came together and of course, once you start sharing, 'Oh I had the same experience'. We were on a high for a long time and, in each other's houses, every waking moment we were active, the word active is very apt ... you couldn't sit still.[66]

The conference structure included the delivery of six papers written by the co-ordinating committee, which included Gerlin, Stella Dadzie, Jocelyn Wolfe, Hansa, and Sylvia Erike.[67] To ensure the conference was truly an autonomous Black women's endeavour, the event's sessions was closed to men and white women. Outside of the hall, Black men operated a crèche and served the refreshments throughout the day in support of the event. The paper's topics were as follows: Black Women and the Law, Black Women and Education, Black Women and Employment, Black Women and Health, and Black Women and the international struggle against

imperialism.[68] The task of delivering these six papers was shared by
the members of the co-ordinating committee. In addition to these
major topics, the conference began with an introduction and a talk
on Black women in Britain. Gerlin opened the conference with
this first session, which included the following reflection on Black
women's leading roles in various sites of struggle, and a rallying call
to unify:

> In the fight for better housing, education and jobs, in the
> campaigns against police harassment, in the struggle for
> a better health service, and in the fight to defend ourselves
> against racist attacks, Black women have constantly been
> in the forefront, making our voices heard and demanding a
> better deal for ourselves and our children.
>
> In the discussion we are about to have, we hope that sisters
> here will talk about their experiences, and tell us about the
> different ways in which they have been organising to fight
> back, so that we can learn from each other, exchange ideas
> and, in the course of the day, genuinely attempt to increase the
> unity among Black sisters here, out of the recognition of the
> undeniable fact that OUR UNITY IS OUR STRENGTH![69]

In addition to these papers the last portion of the conference was
more collaborative, featuring workshops with questions to participants, such as: what major issues should OWAAD take up going
forward, how could OWAAD organise and maintain the national
contacts made at the conference, and how are Black women to
keep in touch with each other to exchange ideas and information
on activities? The conference organisers also called for feedback
from attendees, and the event closed with a film screening of
'Blood of the Condor'.[70] This was a 1969 Bolivian drama about
an indigenous community in Bolivia, who receive medical care
from a peace-corps like organisation that is secretly sterilising the
women of the community. This film certainly bore relevance to the
event, in consideration of Black women's concerns around bodily
autonomy, battles against forced sterilisations and abortions, and
the prevalence of unsafe forms of birth control (in the example of
the Depo-Provera injection, which was largely pushed to Black and

working-class women worldwide, despite not being FDA approved until 1993).[71] The footage of the event was edited into a montage, cuttings from excerpts of the papers being delivered, conversations between the attendees, and debriefs with some of the attendees. This footage lovingly evokes the emotions of the day, and the elation of Gerlin and the other organisers at the end of the event, who were filmed debriefing on the day's proceedings. Gerlin, who by this time had developed an English twang – a clear indication of her rootedness in Britain at this point of her life – exclaimed:

A few sisters came up and said these papers are brilliant!! And they all want copies, and all the journalists and people who are here from other magazines said that they want to write it up and said they'll send it back for criticisms.[72]

The co-ordinating committee also discussed some of the constructive criticism they had received from attendees throughout the day, which included comments that the papers were slightly too long. They also added their own observations, including that there were not as many Asian women present as they would have liked. Indeed, the video footage clearly evidences that the great majority of attendees were women of African and Caribbean descent.[73] These candid discussions between Gerlin and other organisers indicate several things: their surprise at the conference turn out, their excitement that the conference was the start of a significant political undertaking, their earnest practice of self-reflection, and their aims to ensure the activities of OWAAD were representative of the women they sought to involve and inspire. The experience of this conference spurred OWAAD's development, and it soon established committees to ensure that it was non-hierarchical and that the upkeep and progress of the OWAAD was the shared responsibility of represented organisations. Another outcome of the conference was the emergence of dozens more Black women's groups throughout England, and the production of *FOWAAD*, the organisation's news organ.[74] During its lifetime OWAAD organised four annual conferences between 1979 and 1982. Following the triumphant inaugural conference, in 1980 OWAAD organised a conference on the theme of 'Black women fighting back', which was attended by 600 women – clearly OWAAD successfully built on the popularity of its first conference. The buzz that had filled the room of the Abeng Centre in 1979 returned at the second instalment. As the organisers reported, the second conference was an indication of the great progress that had been made in developing this national Black and Asian women's political body:

> For those of us who were involved in organising the first Black women's conference in March 1979, this year's event was a visible example of our progress over the past twelve months … We tried hard to correct the mistakes of last year, and this time we used the conference as a forum for a variety of groups, rather than simply as an opportunity for OWAAD to talk.[75]

Held in Tottenham over two days between 28 and 29 March, the conference included contributions from groups such as the OWAAD central committee (represented by Stella Dadzie); the Abasindi Collective (founded by former members of the Manchester Black Women's Co-operative after a power struggle in late 1979); AWAZ, the first Asian women's collective in the UK; East London Black Women's Organisation; BBWG (represented by Gerlin and Jocelyn); the Black Liberation Front (represented by Pauline Wilson, a leading activist in the movement for prisoner's welfare) and United Black Women's Action Group. Both the BBWG and the Black Liberation Front's contributions to the conference focused on Black women in prisons.[76] Other key topics included discussions around immigration and nationality laws, education, organising around local issues and OWAAD's structure and role. At the third annual conference in 1981 the disparities present in the Black women's movement bubbled to the surface. In this year, OWAAD decided was tasked with addressing the concept of Afro-Asian unity, which OWAAD had worked hard to construct as one of its major organising principles. Another bone of contention was that of lesbianism. In a report from a meeting at the Black Women's Centre on 31 October 1981, OWAAD's central committee was joined by members of Simba Black Women's Group and Southall Black Sisters. As the report noted, the meeting was called to discuss how to 'revive' OWAAD, and stated the need for political discussions between women within OWAAD's network around lesbianism, due to the observation that the tensions surrounding the topic stemmed from people's 'emotional reactions'. As for Afro-Asian unity, the attendees contended that it existed only in principle, and in reality there existed much separation between the two communities. The conclusions from that meeting were that OWAAD should encourage more discussion on both issues.[77] However, despite efforts from OWAAD, which included holding a day's workshop on Afro-Asian unity in February 1981, the cracks would go unrepaired. At OWAAD's fourth and final conference, the theme of 'Black Feminism' proved to be a step too far. Although some groups, such as BBWG and OWAAD's central committee, had come to embrace the term feminism, others were unconvinced of its relevance to Black women, still viewing it as the preserve of the white and apparently bourgeois women's libera-tion movement. This was especially the case for more culturally nationalistic, Pan-African Black groups such as the East London Black Women's Organisation (who instead embraced the term Womanism), and the Black Liberation Front, whose opinion on feminism fluctuated with its membership, but often remained opposed.[78] What is more, a heated debate around sexuality unrav-elled during the conference's proceedings. In addition to the topic of sexuality, which was previously considered as a 'personal' issue over a political one, there were other such topics which gained a higher precedence in the 1980s. For example, workshops around mixed-'race' identity, culture, family, and sexuality more broadly would have not appeared as priorities in earlier years. In compar-ison to the first conference of 1979, which focused on Black women's various struggles with state racism as well as the wider anti-imperialist struggle, this was a notable divergence from the political agenda that was present during the rise of the organisa-tion. Indeed, the only topic from 1979 to have survived into 1982 was that of Black women and health.[79] In conjunction with this, the women who had put so much work into establishing OWAAD and maintaining it were themselves evolving and seeking out new pastures. Gerlin's departure from England to Zimbabwe in 1983 coincided with OWAAD's disintegration. As Beverley Bryan reflected, the amount of issues presented to OWAAD's central committee proved too great for a small network of women to respond to, and others failed to take up the challenge:

> I felt a lot of the time it was because we were like the founder members. All the problems became ours to solve and I suppose I got tired of it. I felt I wasn't growing, but I was being drained by it.[80]

As an unfunded group, OWAAD was fuelled by the energies of its organisers who, after years of continuous struggle, were understandably burned out. In reflective discussions on sustaining Black community projects, some argued that funding grants could provide longevity and stability. As OWAAD steered clear of state funding, this could be considered a possible contributor to the burnout of its key activists.[81] There were other factors too, not least that the organisation was established within a specific political context that later shifted, as evidenced by the changing nature of its conference themes. For what had been such a substantial, influential and ambitious project, some believe that OWAAD's history has been tainted by an obsessive interest in its demise, and accusations of homophobic tendencies in the Black women's movement.[82] For its main organisers, the demise of OWAAD had much more to do with an organic repositioning which reflected wider trends in Black community politics, including, for instance, the dissipation of political blackness as a unifying strategy, ideological differences between Black women's groups, and the closing of one historical chapter to begin another.[83] This viewpoint is shared by Gerlin:

> There were contradictions, there were conflicts, the women's movement also had its internal contradictions and different issues. Some were resolved, some left unresolved, and perhaps they are still going on, but that's the way we move. We are not static, there's a movement always, so therefore the struggle continues.[84]

NOTES

1 Gerlin Bean, 'No, We Didn't Burn Our Bras', in Hilary Robertson-Hickling (ed), *That Time in Foreign*, Hansib, 2016, p155.
2 For a survey of Black women's organisations throughout Britain, see

Julia Sudbury, 'Other Kinds of Dreams': Black Women's Organisations and the Politics of Transformation, Routledge, 1998.

3   Zainab Abbas interviewed by the author and Hakim Adi, 8 April 2021, p8.

4   Ibid, p15.

5   Gerlin Bean, 'Do you remember Olive Morris? Oral History Project', Lambeth Archives: IV/279, p2; hereafter DYROM.

6   Beverley Bryan, 'Tales from the Struggle', www.youtube.com, 5 June 2020.

7   Gail Lewis in Brenna Bhandar and Rafeef Ziadah (eds), Revolutionary Feminisms: Conversations on Collective Action and Radical Thought, Verso: London and New York, 2020, p60.

8   Robin Bunce and Paul Field, Darcus Howe: A Political Biography, Bloomsbury, 2013, p149.

9   Selma James, 'Wages for Housework: 50 years of campaigning – Selma James, founder of the WFH Campaign, in conversation with Margaret Prescod, co-founder Black Women for Wages for Housework', globalwomenstrike.net.

10 Selma James, 'Women, the Unions and Work, Or … What is Not to Be Done', Notting Hill Women's Liberation Workshop Group: London, 1972, p2.

11 Ibid.

12 Zainab Abbas interviewed by the author, 8 April 2021.

13 Black Women's Group, Speak Out, Vol 1, No 1, c. 1977, p3; hereafter BWG.

14 Bean DYROM, op cit, p2.

15 Melba Wilson, interviewed by the author, 3 June 2022, pp2-3.

16 Gail Lewis, 'Heart of the Race: Oral Histories of the Black Women's Movement', Black Cultural Archives: ORAL/1/21, pp8-9; hereafter BCA.

17 Programme of 'Politics and the Women's Movement', Polytechnic of Central London, LSE: 7SHRA/A/2, box 1, folder 2.

18 Sheila Rowbotham, Daring to Hope: My Life in the 1970s, Verso: London, 2021, p185.

19 Natalie Thomlinson, Race, Ethnicity and the Women's Movement in England, 1968-1993, Palgrave Macmillan, 2016, p67.

20 A.S. Francis, 'A Luta Continua: The political journey of Manchester's Black women activists, 1945-1980', in Hakim Adi (ed), Many Struggles: New Histories of African and Caribbean People in Britain, Pluto Press: London, 2023; Photograph: Official opening of the Manchester Black Women's Co-operative in 1974, Greater Manchester Record Office, Ref: 1741/11.

21 Francis, op cit.
22 Beverley Bryan, 'From migrant to settler and the making of a Black community: An autoethnographic account', *African and Black Diaspora: An International Journal*, 2020, p192.
23 Beverley Bryan, Stella Dadzie and Suzanne Scafe, *Heart of the Race: Black Women's Lives in Britain*, Virago: London, 1985, p150.
24 See several anonymous testimonies in Bryan, Dadzie and Scafe, op cit. See also 'The Heart of the Race: Oral Histories of the Black Women's Movement', BCA.
25 Bryan, Dadzie and Scafe, op cit, pp143-144.
26 Beverley Bryan interviewed by the author, 7 March 2023.
27 Zainab Abbas interviewed by the author, 8 April 2021, p8; p17.
28 Sheila Rowbotham, *Daring to Hope: My Life in the 1970s*, Verso: London, 2021, p27.
29 Wilson, op cit, p6.
30 Gail Lewis interviewed by the author, 3rd June 2022, p11.
31 Stella Dadzie, 'The Heart of the Race: Oral Histories of the Black Women's Movement', BCA: ORAL/1/12, pp17-18.
32 Stella Dadzie interviewed by the author, 25 July 2019, pp8-9.
33 Olive Gallimore quoted in Thomlinson, op cit, p86.
34 BWG, *Speak Out*, Vol 1, No 1, p9, c. 1977.
35 Ibid.
36 The estimated date 1977 is because Olive Morris visited China and wrote the report 'A Sister's Visit to China' in the same year, which is featured in *Speak Out*'s first issue.
37 For more analysis on *Speak Out* and other Black Women's newsletters, see Tracy Fisher, *What's Left of Blackness: Feminisms, Transracial Solidarities, and the Politics of Belonging in Britain*, Palgrave Macmillan: London, 2012 and Milo Miller (ed), *Speak Out!: The Brixton Black Women's Group*, Verso: London, 2023.
38 BWG, 'Editorial', and 'Scrap SUS now', in *Speak Out*, No 2, undated.
39 *Outwrite*, No 1, March 1982 – No 71, December 1988, LSE Library.
40 BWG, 'Memories of Olive: A Very Strong and Fearless Sister', *Speak Out*, No 3, 1980, pp9-10; 'In Memory of Sylvia Ome Erike', *Speak Out,* No 5, December 1983, pp17-18.
41 Zainab Abbas interviewed by the author, 8 April 2021, p6.
42 Colin A. Beckles, '"We Shall Not Be Terrorized Out of Existence": The Political Legacy of England's Black Bookshops', *Journal of Black Studies*, Vol 29, No 1, September 1998, pp51-72.
43 *Speak Out*, No 1, quoted in Lucy Delap, 'Feminist Bookshops, Reading Cultures and the Women's Liberation Movement in Great Britain, c. 1974-2000', *History Workshop Journal*, No 81, Spring 2016, p181.

44 Jocelyn Wolfe, 'Sisterhood and After: the Women's Liberation Oral History Project', British Library: C1420.

45 Hansard – UK Parliament, Ubran Programmes (Government Aid), api.parliament.uk/historic-hansard/commons/1968/jul/22/urban-programmes-government-aid, 22 July 1968.

46 Gerlin Bean, 'The Heart of the Race: Oral Histories of the Black Women's Movement', 2009, BCA: ORAL/1/3, p44.

47 Keith Tompson, *Under Siege: Racism and Violence in Britain Today*, Penguin Books: London, 1988, pp94-95.

48 Ibid.

49 Ibid.

50 'Editorial', *ELBWO*, No 1, 1983.

51 Diana Watt and Adele D. Jones, *Catching Hell and Doing Well: Black women in the UK – The Abasindi Collective*, Trentham Books, 2015, p39.

52 Bean 2009, op cit, p45.

53 BWG, *Speak Out*, No 3, 1980, p1.

54 Marlene T. Bogle, 'Brixton Black Women's Centre: Organizing on Child Sexual Abuse', *Feminist Review*, No 28, January 1988, p132.

55 Ibid.

56 Ibid, p133.

57 Ibid.

58 Bean 2016, op cit, p156.

59 BWG, *Speak Out*, No 4, 1982, p14.

60 Bean 2016, op cit, p156.

61 BWG, *Speak Out*, 'Editorial: on Black Women Organising', No 5, 1983, p2.

62 Bean 2016, op cit, p156.

63 Bean DYROM, op cit, p14.

64 Bryan et al, op cit.

65 Organisation of Women of Asian and African Descent (OWAAD) conference, 18 March 1979, BCA: Recording/154.

66 Ama Gueye, 'The Heart of the Race: Oral Histories of the Black Women's Movement', BCA: ORAL/1/16, p34.

67 OWAAD, Letter to sisters, 30 March 1979, BCA: MCKENLEY/1/1.

68 'National Black Women's Conference' (NBWC), BCA: MCKENLEY/1/1.

69 OWAAD conference, 18 March 1979, BCA: Recording/154.

70 NBWC, BCA: MCKENLEY/1/1.

71 'The Campaign Against Depo-Provera', BCA: DADZIE 1/9.

72 OWAAD conference, 18 March 1979, BCA: Recording/154.

73 Ibid.

74 Brixton Black Women's Group, 'Black Women Organising', *Feminist Review*, No 17, Autumn, 1984, pp84-85.

75 'Black Women Fighting Back', *Spare Rib*, c. 1981, p49.

76 'Contributions from groups', BCA: DADZIE 1/1/17.

77 OWAAD, 'Minutes for the meeting of the [?] at the Black Women's Centre', 31 October 1981.

78 'Which Way Forward for OWAAD: Statement of the Black Liberation Front', *Grassroots*, Oct/Nov 1982. BCA: LIBFRONT.

79 OWAAD, 'timetable', (c. 1982), BCA: DADZIE/1/8/3

80 Bryan, 'The Heart of the Race: Oral Histories of the Black Women's Movement', BCA: ORAL/1/8, pp19-20.

81 Sudbury, op cit, pp12-13.

82 See Thomlinson, op cit, pp203-4.

83 For more on these political changes, see Rosie Wild, '"Black was the colour of our fight." Black Power in Britain, 1955-1976', PhD thesis, University of Sheffield, 2013; John Narayan, 'British Black Power: The anti-imperialism of political blackness and the problem of nativist socialism', *The Sociological Review*, Vol 67, No 5, September 2019.

84 Bean 2016, op cit, p157.

6

The struggle continues
wherever you are

Imperialism/colonialism/neo-colonialism has had such a
stranglehold on us that I don't know which generation will
emerge from this deluge. There is no place to "escape" to if
that's what one is trying to do. I am really missing you all
... Take care. Love and sisterhood. The struggle continues
wherever you are.[1]

As the Black radical movement in Britain lost momentum by
the 1980s, Gerlin began to contemplate her next sites of
struggle. The movement suffered a sharp decline in revolutionary
fervour, due in large part to the state's successful pacification of
Black community projects. Black radicalism was also affected by the
wider societal shift toward neoliberalism. As has been addressed by
commentators such as A. Sivanandan, although it became more
apparent in the aftermath of the 1981 uprisings, this shift had been
underway for some time before that. It could be identified in the
work of the Community Relations Councils and Community
Relations Commissions, which sought to act as bridges between
disenfranchised, racialised communities and the State.[2] After 1981,
this became more obvious in the prevalance of the term 'ethnic
minorities' in the place of other descriptors such as Black or Asian,
and the emergence of equality and diversity job roles.[3] For those
like Gerlin who had not envisioned staying in Britain for long in
the first instance, this development signalled that the time had
come to seek out new horizons in the revolutionary struggle outside
the confines of Britain and the West. For some this resulted in the

decision to return to their homeland, and for others this meant relocating to newly independent nations on the African continent, where they may or may not have had familial ties but certainly had political ones. Gerlin did both from 1983 and into the 2000s. First she took a job in Zimbabwe in 1983, where she resided until 1987, and thereafter returned to Jamaica where she remained until very recently. As we saw in the previous chapter, Gerlin's departure from Britain coincided with the end of an era in Britain's Black women's movement. By the time of her move to Zimbabwe Gerlin had resided in England for twenty-five years, and her work as a tireless activist in the spheres of Black radicalism, feminism, community and youth work had a lasting impact. In some ways the Britain she left behind differed greatly from the one she had arrived to as an eighteen year old student nurse, and in other ways it did not. By 1983 Britain's economy was being ravaged by neoliberal policies. The public sector – most notably the NHS – was on life support.[4] Police brutality and racist immigration policies remained persistent problems. The revolutionary optimism of the late 1960s and early 1970s had dissipated. And although the legacy of the prior decades of struggle had survived, the various initiatives and programmes which Gerlin and others had worked so hard to establish either folded or transformed into different manifestations. For example, the Abeng Centre, reinvented as Karibu, still exists today, running a supplementary school and alternative education for thirteen to sixteen-year olds who have been permanently excluded from mainstream school.[5] The Brixton Black Women's Group, however, ceased activity in 1985, and the Black Women's Centre closed its doors in 1989.[6] After her move from Britain, despite the physical separation from the Black radical network she had helped to cultivate there, Gerlin continued her commitment to Black liberation activism. But Gerlin's absence from her community in Britain, with whom she had built so many important projects, waged significant political battles, and cultivated lifelong bonds, was not without personal difficulty. This section is focused on exploring this distinct chapter of Gerlin's life, looking at her activities in Zimbabwe and subsequently Jamaica, asking whether she was able to transfer the type of work she had conducted during the 1970s to Zimbabwe and Jamaica, how much tangible progress she witnessed after such an intensive period of struggle in Zimbabwe, what challenges the new nation faced in its early years, and Gerlin's analysis of the situation there. In addition, we are also interested in which sections of the two nations' populations remained the most marginalised and oppressed in the post-colonial context, and how Gerlin reacted to their specific problems.

In January 1983, three years after Zimbabwe emerged victorious from a fifteen-year-long armed struggle for liberation against white minority rule, Gerlin left London to contribute to the newly independent nation's onerous task of nation-building. As a longstanding anti-imperialist, Gerlin and other participants in Britain's Black radical movement had been invested in Africa's liberation struggles while they were ongoing, both politically as well as emotionally. As mentioned in the previous chapter, the Black Women's Movement had links with African women liberation fighters, including those active in Zimbabwe's struggle for independence. For Gerlin, the decision to move to Zimbabwe was therefore a natural progression, as she later explained: 'The next phase of my life was in 1983 when, after we did so much support for Zimbabwe and now it was "free", we thought, I decided to be a volunteer in Zimbabwe to see what I had to offer'.[7] Zimbabwe was one of the last European colonial outposts in Africa, apart from South Africa and Namibia, which remained under the yoke of apartheid until the 1990s. The liberation struggle had come to an end after the Lancaster House Agreement in December 1979, where representatives of the liberation organisations and the interim Zimbabwe-Rhodesian government agreed on the need for a general election and universal suffrage. A subsequent election resulted in a victory for ZANU-PF under Robert Mugabe. The Lancaster House Agreement, in bringing an end to the armed struggle, resulted in a new constitution, which led to Mugabe's proclamation of the process of reconciliation. This, from the outset, limited the degree to which radical change could be made, and safeguarded the interests of white settlers. It also created a contradiction as one of the rallying calls during the liberation struggle was for land redistribution for African Zimbabweans, but this was largely prohibited by the property rights for white settlers – one of the key features of the constitution outlined at Lancaster House.[8] In any case, Zimbabwean independence represented a new hope for people of African heritage in the diaspora, as well as those on the continent. However, the complex realities of post-independence nation building, and the government's gradual shift away from its revolutionary principles, soon revealed themselves.

CATHOLIC INSTITUTE OF INTERNATIONAL RELATIONS

The opportunity of a post for Gerlin in Zimbabwe came via the Catholic Institute of International Relations (CIIR), which organised programmes for volunteers to put forward their skills and participate in the process of reconstruction. As a non-governmental organisation (NGO), much of the work of the CIIR had no religious focus. Many young leftists and radicals in Britain were attracted to the CIIR and the opportunities it provided for a route into volunteering. The CIIR was originally founded as The Sword of the Spirit in 1940, in response to Hitler's rejection of 'kinship and love'. Its founding principles were to promote Catholicism across the globe, and to encourage peace and democracy. It had an anti-racist, anti-colonial orientation and aimed to support Catholics in Britain in their 'determination to build a peace upon this new concept of the world as a global neighbourhood'.[9] As the organisation developed, it took up a number of priorities that related back to the task of developing a 'global neighbourhood' or 'community', including opposing acts of repression both in Britain and abroad, notably in South America, southern Africa and South East Asia. Within Britain the CIIR worked on challenging racism and discrimination, and partnered with the Africa Centre on race relations projects.[10] During the liberation struggle in Zimbabwe, the CIIR had supported opposition to white minority rule and human rights abuses of the country's subjugated African population. Then, upon independence in 1980, the CIIR opened a secular volunteering programme, with a particular focus on education, disability support and rehabilitation for ex-combatants.[11] Gerlin's role was as a programme coordinator, and as such she was in charge of supervising volunteers and their projects in the areas of education and health. She flew out to Zimbabwe in January of 1983, on what started as a two-year contract and became a four-year commitment.

As programme coordinator Gerlin lived in the capital, Harare, for the majority of the time, though she regularly visited the volunteers, who were stationed mainly in rural areas.[12] On her living conditions, Gerlin commented: 'We tried to work and live at the same level as the people. So I didn't live in palatial surroundings, which you could as the coordinator. The volunteers lived on-site at the school or in the hospital, and we re-trained them'.[13] The overall aim was to set up various programmes for the benefit of communities, and in particular rural communities, to help prevent 'rural flight' to urban areas. The volunteers worked on two-year contracts, building projects that would then be taken over by Zimbabweans: 'The other thing we did was we asked the government to pay each one a salary as they would pay their own person who was coming back. My idea was that when a trained Zimbabwean came back they would replace that and there must be a salary for that person, for the Zimbabwean'.[14] Gerlin was charged with providing the volunteers with a three-month orientation. Throughout her four years, she supervised roughly thirty volunteers, who she recalled were 'English, young, kind of socialist, radical people who had also participated in England in the struggle and they came through this organisation'.[15] At the time of her move Gerlin had gained a considerable reputation among Britain's Black and women's liberation enclaves. By February 1983 she was forty-four and had over thirteen years' experience in activism. However, from the available evidence it seems the volunteers she worked with were unaware of this aspect of her life. One of the volunteers under her coordination, Hugh MacCamley, recalled that she didn't discuss her activities in Britain, and most conversations either related to their volunteer programmes or brief stories about their families and lives back home. In any case, Gerlin made a strong impression. She quickly gained his admiration for her aptness in the coordinator role, in addition to her astute understanding of the conditions under which they were working:

> I honestly had no idea that she was working in any activist associations. I knew very little about her background, I'd been told very little in England. So that enabled me to meet her and make my own impressions, and I thought she was abso-

lutely suited, totally, to the coordinator's role in a country that
was really struggling to find its feet and its identity after all
those years of colonial rule ... I found her to be very good
humoured ... There were many occasions in the first few
weeks when we were doing what we humorously called 'diso-
rientation'. Because you learn a lot of things, but it's not until
you're alone on your own project that you realise the orientation really begins then ... But Gerlin was very good, she had
a good sense of reality of things which was important for us.
I had absolutely no idea about her experiences before that. I
learned all that afterwards, and much more since ... But I
found her very practical, pragmatic, human, and humane.[16]

In her later recollections, Gerlin spoke positively of her experience
in the job and of working with the volunteers: 'It was hard work
but it gave me a lot of opportunity to develop certain programmes.
We worked throughout the country and we had volunteers coming
in ... The volunteers came and we trained them, but they were
all high-powered people. There were doctors, because those were
the areas of need. There were teachers, educators and there were
project development officers, meaning rural engineering people
and so on'.[17] Hugh MacCamley also recalled a heartening experience he and Gerlin shared together when he accompanied her to
a hospital to check on a doctor's programme and they witnessed
a baby being born.[18] However, there were some challenges to the
job. One of them was having to navigate several instances where
female volunteers fell pregnant during their contract, which threw
up complications on the basis of racial politics. Gerlin, who was
supervising a team of white, English professionals, was aware that
some of the women were engaging in romantic relationships with
Zimbabwean men, which she suggested was sometimes driven
by their desire for a 'brown' baby.[19] On one occasion Gerlin was
verbally abused by the mother of a volunteer, who was incensed
that her daughter was pregnant by a Zimbabwean: 'Poor little me
– there were all white, high-powered people, and I'm supposed to
keep them in line and supervise them. Well I wasn't able to because
they were all adults. I remember one girl, she was a doctor, a big
woman – she had a relationship with an ex-combatant and she got

pregnant. Several of them did, they wanted brown babies, so what can you do? The mother called me on the phone and I said, "Yes Mrs. X, how can I help you?" She said, "You let them rape my daughter and now she's pregnant!" I said, 'Rape? Beg your pardon? She's thirty-three, she's a medical doctor, she's living with the man and she's pregnant for him and you tell me that I allowed it? What have I got to do with it? Lady, get off the phone!'"[20] These situations clearly irritated Gerlin – no doubt they were not the kind of tasks she thought she was signing up for. Writing to her comrade and close friend Stella Dadzie back in London, Gerlin confided in her: 'The volunteers themselves are a problem. Two of the women are pregnant and want to have the babies (for Black men of course). I had to fly another one back to England for an abortion a couple of weeks ago. These are "matured adults" so called who come to help "third world" development, sometimes I wonder what the fuck I am doing in this job. What a price to pay just to be in Africa'.[21]

POLITICS IN ZIMBABWE

Outside of her daily tasks as coordinator, Gerlin was grappling with the political trends and developments taking place in the first years of Zimbabwe's independence. During the four years she lived there, Gerlin witnessed a number of significant turning points that both affected her on a personal level and also moved her to theorise these situations in the context of the wider trends in global politics during the last decades of the twentieth century. She identified at least one of three key themes within each significant event that took place. The first theme was what she referred to as tribalism, in particular the complex dynamic between the Shona community, who form the majority of Zimbabwe's population, and the Ndebele community, who form Zimbabwe's largest minority group. During the struggle against colonialism and white minority rule, the shared goals and nationalist ideals for a free, unified and African-led Zimbabwe provided a sense of unity, though the struggle still featured political rifts. But from 1980 onwards this began to unravel. The struggle to end colonial rule is also referred to as the Second Chimurenga, in tribute to the legacy of Zimbabwe's first war of independence against British colonialism, fought between 1896 and 1897.[22] During the First Chimurenga, Ndebele and Shona people came together to revolt against the encroachment of the British South Africa company on their land. Throughout the period of European colonial rule in Africa, colonial governments worked to sow divisions between African peoples, and post-independence it proved challenging to overcome these conditions. Throughout the Second Chimurenga, ZANU-PF and ZAPU emerged as the two dominant organisations, representing the militant and revolutionary factions of the independence movement. Following independence, being a supporter of ZAPU and a member of the Ndebele community was viewed as synonymous, creating a rift between the ZANU-PF government and Ndebele communities.[23]

A second important trend in newly independent Zimbabwe was the question of women's liberation and the position of women in society in general. It is estimated that during the Second Chimurenga around 10,000 women participated as combatants in ZANU-PF's armed wing, ZANLA.[24] A large number of women were also present in ZAPU and its armed wing ZIPRA, and both organisations argued that women's participation was essential for the nation's liberation. As ZAPU literature at the time attested, women existed in all areas of the liberation struggle, from the military to political and economic strategy: 'Zimbabwean women have been playing a major role too in the fight for their country's freedom. They have joined their men in large numbers and assumed active roles at various levels of their national organisation'.[25] Indeed, the liberation movement was key in changing attitudes toward gender equality, as Robert Mugabe later recalled: 'We learned throughout the liberation struggle that success and power are possible when men and women are united as equals'.[26] The majority of women who participated in these movements were unmarried women and teenage girls who, through their experiences in armed struggle, subverted traditional perceptions of women's roles.[27] As the struggle developed, women and Zimbabwean revolutionaries as a whole viewed women's liberation and national liberation as intrinsically interlinked. In comparison to other liberation struggles, for example those being waged in Namibia and Mozambique, Zimbabwean women participated in a larger number, and therefore became a source of inspiration for women's movements across the globe, including the Black women's movement in Britain.[28] Zimbabwe's liberation movement was not alone in this, indeed all African liberation struggles expressed the necessity for a revolution within a revolution, to transform the subjugated position of women into one of full participation and empowerment.[29] Taking all of this into account, it's perhaps not surprising then that Gerlin had high aspirations for the future of women's rights in Zimbabwe, as did Zimbabwean women themselves, whether or not they were ex-combatants. But as we will see, while there were some efforts by the government to pass progressive legislation for women, patriarchal sentiments were far from eradicated. The third important part of Gerlin's time in Zimbabwe relates to the overall political condition of Zimbabwe following the Lancaster House Agreement, and the ZANU-PF government's evolution post-independence. Throughout the Second Chimurenga and beyond, ZANU-PF espoused socialist beliefs. During the liberation struggle it was heavily inspired by Marxist-Leninism, but even more so by Maoism. Despite the great intensity of the liberation struggle, it came to a close with a compromise. In the aftermath, although the government continued its revolutionary rhetoric, many revolutionaries were met with disappointment. The air of optimism from 1980 slowly began to dissipate. Having left Britain in a bid to continue with radical Black organising, Gerlin had to grapple with these challenges during her time in Zimbabwe. By now a respected political theorist, she began to relate them to a wider revolutionary struggle, which she sought to continue it this new environment.

Gerlin's reactions to political developments during the early years of reconstruction in Zimbabwe are captured in a substantial collection of letters she wrote to Stella Dadzie in the years she spent there. These letters have been carefully preserved by Stella and are in the process of being catalogued at the Black Cultural Archives.[30] Given the deep trust and bond that Gerlin and Stella had developed over the years, the letters provide us with a considerable insight into Gerlin's candid thoughts and opinions. The topics featured in the letters suggest that the correspondence between these two friends was a lifeline for Gerlin, filling a void in political discussion that she had become so accustomed to in Britain's Black movement, but which she hadn't been able to replicate among others in her new environment. The first letter was written just five weeks after she had arrived in the country, on 14 February 1983. Perhaps understandably, Gerlin was immediately struck by a grave disappointment in the lack of transformation in Zimbabwe since independence, and she feared what this meant for African people on the continent and in the diaspora, in a supposedly 'postcolonial' climate. Gerlin was already picking up on the tensions between the Ndebele and Shona communities, the build-up of tribalism, and ZANU-PF's justification for state repression of 'dissenters' in the Ndebele-dominated area of Matebeleland in the southern region of Zimbabwe. Gerlin was also struck by the presence of Western-educated individuals occupying leadership positions, and what she viewed as the bourgeois attitudes of women she encountered, which posed a barrier to her becoming part of a politicised community of Black women there. There were also the effects of South Africa's ongoing apartheid regime and its influence on Zimbabwe, as well as the rapidly growing presence of Westerners:

Dear Stella,

It's 5 weeks now since I have been in this country, and I am finding it very difficult to really adjust to the situation, hence my reluctance in writing. It's like a bad dream come through [sic] not from a personal point of view, but in terms of what is happening in the country as a whole. All my hopes are really shattered and I am beginning to feel that there is no real future for the Black race ... Zimbabwe the land of hope is hope-less. After such long suffering and struggles people haven't learnt anything. The govt is full with so called comrades who have returned from the West, with all their Western values which they have set about imposing on the people. If something doesn't give there will be a civil war soon, between the Ndebele and the Shona speaking people, because tribalism is being used as a scapegoat for lots of bad planning and govt compromise. It would appear, at least on the surface, but I feel more fundamentally that a policy of reconciliation doesn't work in the interest of the Black people, although the white Rhodesians are benefitting ... The other danger is the amount of expats that the govt are bringing who fucks [sic] up the works even more, get govt salary and have a good time. If you take education, there are Canadians, Brits, Aussies, etc. etc. in fact the rest of the world is here. They are given status and the Zimbabweans, the real people who have suffered aren't given a chance. Clearly I don't know what the hell I am doing here. I don't want to contribute to this mess, so I have to think clearly before I do anything. So my sister, I am just trying to meet people and to observe the scene. One can't be critical without a very clear understanding of the contradictions that are at play ... I find myself driving around, or riding a bicycle which is quite good for me, but I can't relax I need some action, things here seem very laid back. And everyone is on the booze. I met a few women the other day, but they are not aware of their oppression. These are however your aspiring petit bourgeois. So I am really missing you all. I already feel isolated – no political stimulation so far. Take care.

Love and sisterhood. The struggle continues wherever you are.

Gerlin[31]

This candid communication from Gerlin highlights the sisterhood between her and Stella, exemplifying the strong bonds that were forged between Black women during the most intensive years of radical organising in Britain. Evidently, what she was faced with upon arrival in Zimbabwe was far from what she had hoped for or envisioned. Although clearly stressed and deeply disappointed by this, Gerlin's years of political education and training in Britain's Black movement and as a part of the anti-imperialist struggle gave her the ability to analyse the major political and social issues facing Zimbabwe as a newly independent nation. In her subsequent letters her revolutionary optimism seemed to gradually return, although several months into her stay she remained unsure of the decision to take up the post. When she wrote again in April 1983, the physical separation from her comrades was beginning to take its toll, and she reported that 'on several occasions I felt like just packing my bags and returning to the people who I love and trust. However I am beginning to feel more positive about what I want to do and how to do it'.[32] Her letters consisted of summaries of recent developments, including the latest events in what became known as the Gukurahundi, considered by some as a genocide against citizens in Matabeleland at the hands of the government between 1983 and 1987.[33] From Gerlin's perspective, the context behind these events consisted of four elements, all underpinned by a frustration at the lack of progress caused by the policy of reconciliation: 'My own perception of the situation is something like this; with the govt policy of reconciliation many people i.e. the masses or sections of the masses were really pissed off as not much was being changed for them ... the result was in the 1st instance people who waged the armed struggle began to dissent ... The 2nd problem was when arms were found on so-called ZAPU's or Nkomo's farm, and his dismissal from govt. This created a 2nd group of dissenters who are Nkomo's followers, who felt that Mugabe and ZANU wanted to run the whole show. So what you had were fightings in the army between ZANU and ZAPU comrades. The 3rd element in this saga are the South Africans who used the split between the two groups, to step up their infiltration and their programme of destabilisation. And 4th you have the masses of unemployed who like any other country some turn to crime'.[34] Indeed, these letters are as much vital, first-hand accounts of significant historical moments in Zimbabwe post-independence as they are a useful records for sketching Gerlin's biography.

WOMEN, POLITICS AND ORGANISING IN THE 'NEW DAWN'

As two staunch Black socialist feminists, much of Gerlin and Stella Dadzie's correspondence concentrated on analysing the specific issues of women in post-independence Zimbabwean society. There has been much historical reflection on this, by female ex-combatants as well as historians.[35] The consensus from both is that, despite the promising rhetoric on women's rights during the liberation struggle, and an increase in progressive notions on the capabilities of women as equal participants in the fight for independence, once that struggle was won little materially changed for women. Society reverted back to pre-independence patriarchal and colonial structures as they pertained to women. Despite the lack of fundamental change, there was of course important progress as a result of independence. The emergence of an African-led state meant that African women benefited from new legislation, such as the Equal Pay Regulations Act of 1980, Legal Age of Majority Act of 1982, Labour Relations Act of 1984, and Matrimonial Causes Act in 1985.[36]

In April 1983 Gerlin wrote to Stella that 'women here are still in the same position as before'.[37] She hadn't been able to scope out the terrain of Black women's organising by this time, having been focused on getting situated in her new job role. It is worth considering that within CIIR Gerlin was working amongst white volunteers, and thus wouldn't have been able to utilise her work connections to build a Black women's project. She therefore had to look outside of her day-to-day work. In addition, she was also new to the particular way sexism and misogyny manifested in Zimbabwe, and took time to observe it as a newcomer: 'I haven't checked out where the Black women are as of yet, those who I have met so far are the petit bourgeois, [interested in] hip Western fashion and competition for men. Wife beating is the [flavour] of the day, and polygamy around … Jeans aren't allowed in certain places, the sexism is so crude that I need to know more of the language to really deal with it in an effective way'.[38] Months later, in August 1983, Gerlin came across other Caribbean women, and here she discovered a hierarchy within Zimbabwe's Black population, stating that the Caribbean women were 'as reactionary as the whites, with their "domestic workers" or "my girl" or "my gardener". They treat big men and women with no respect. The exploitation continues now by us Blacks, when will it end'.[39] In the same vein, Gerlin also reported on her attempts to form an organisation of Caribbeans based in Zimbabwe as a political project, which appears to have been fruitless, though not for lack of trying. Gerlin's greatest challenge in resurrecting her activism and encouraging others to take up political organising had more to do with the political landscape in postcolonial Africa. A surge of middle-class people from the African diaspora moving into Zimbabwe's urban areas proved to be far from a receptive audience, even in the context of the US invasion of Grenada in October 1983:

> Well what can I say, it's nearly a year since I am here, and still I can't really get into the vibes of this place ... I tried with a few others to start a Zimbabwe Caribbean Association, I didn't realise that people could be so reactionary coming from those parts. They wouldn't support me, in a statement to the press about Grenada or a petition to the American embassy so I told them where to get off ... I am going back to keep up the fight. The most reactionary ones will eventually leave, and there are a few who would be influenced. I have to work out some tactics.[40]

Despite Gerlin's conviction, it does not appear that any such project was ever set up during her time in Zimbabwe. A watershed moment with regards to women in Zimbabwe was 'Operation Clean-Up', which took place between October and November 1983. This operation was conducted by the police force, who utilised a pre-independence vagrancy law in an attempt to repress African women's freedoms in urban areas under the guise of protecting the nation's 'morality'.[41] Any unescorted woman seen after 6 p.m. could be accused of prostitution and arrested. Once detained, their release was dependent on their ability to prove that they were married by presenting a marriage certificate. This posed multiple problems. First, any women who were single or had married in a traditional rather than civil ceremony would not have any way of disproving that they were sex workers. Second, while there was widespread public outrage about this operation, the outrage was due to the indiscriminate nature of the round-up, and there was very little criticism of its premise.[42] Third, Operation Clean-Up was but one aspect of a widespread moral panic around women's sexuality and agency. Both before and after this operation, the national press was filled with vitriol about women, with claims that African women, particularly ex-combatants, were becoming too promiscuous, and were to blame for rising cases of sexually transmitted diseases and 'baby dumping' on doorsteps.[43] Gerlin recounted Operation Clean-Up to Stella Dadzie, framing it as part of a wider trend of repression of women. She also reported on her encounters with (and challenges to) state officials, in particular military officer Solomon Mujuru, also known as Rex Nhongo. While she aimed to highlight the systemic issues faced by women that needed addressing, her advice was ignored:

> The repression of human rights gets worse daily especially as it concerns women. The latest attack is rounding up prostitutes. The way it's done here is that if you are unescorted after 6pm, then you are a prostitute, so you are picked up. By the police and army and taken to jail … This whole anti-women campaign started with the *Herald* which is the daily paper, accusing women of spreading V.D. Then the next thing was women 'dumping babies' and how you can't walk on the streets without a man after dark, and it gets dark here about 6pm. As far as the ministry of community development and women's affairs is concerned the move to clean up prostitution is welcomed. What they seem to forget is that not all women want a man or not all women who [are] on the streets after 6pm are prostitutes. Last night I met the chairperson who is heading the clean up squad. He is the chief commander of the army, Rex Nhongo, and his wife is the minister for women's affairs, can you believe it? The guy is an ass. I really let him have a piece of my mind on the situation. He asked me to give him the solution to the problem, which I did, by telling him to stop breaking up families, improve the conditions for women, in terms of asking the government to give women a decent wage. In this era of drought, to make sure women and children have enough food, water and a decent place to live. If they concentrate on things like that, although they will never eradicate prostitution women would not have to sell themselves for a few dollars because they are destitute. He was so drunk I don't know if any of it went in.[44]

The above accounts from Gerlin demonstrate her attempts to cultivate a political community in Zimbabwe and to intervene in instances whereby women's rights were being stripped away. But it is clear that these efforts had limited effect. Unlike her success in recruiting for the Black women's movement in Britain, Gerlin did not find a responsive atmosphere for her activism in Zimbabwe. Naturally, this isolation and lack of political stimulation weighed down on her over the four-year period she lived there. During Operation Clean-Up, she grappled with an internal struggle over not only the situation in the country at that time, but her own position in all of it:

> I am riddled with contradictions. The love hate saga, of wanting to be here, at the same time wishing it could be different. So I don't really know what the future will bring. Right now I feel I couldn't live in England again at the same time this is not really where I want to be either. What a state to be in on the eve of being 45 (smile).[45]

The attitudes Gerlin came across were not all disheartening, however. One aspect of her work that provided a refreshing experience was her travels to rural areas, where she came across different women to those she encountered in the capital: 'most of my other time is taken up travelling around visiting volunteers in projects or looking for new projects for them, so I am out in the rural areas quite a lot. I love it when I go to these places. The people, especially the women are so different, real people, not those "plastics" I meet in Harare'.[46] A year later, in October 1984, Gerlin's conviction for the necessity to involve herself in a political project in Zimbabwe remained the same. But while she continued attempts to forge connections, she became disenchanted with her programme coordinating work, the work of NGO and aid organisations more generally. As she relayed to Stella:

> Well my dear I am here stagnating, politically, culturally and economically. Zimbabwe is a very difficult place to get involved into. One thing I learn more and more is how aid works and how dangerous it all is, and still how difficult it is for a newly independent state to survive without it. My dear it's catch 22, corruption is rife but they are trying their

'darndest' to route [sic] it out. All the contradictions are very clear, a leadership code came out of the ZANU congress, but how it will be implemented is another story. The struggle is on for a one party state elections next year will be very interesting to watch. The whites are getting more entrenched. Many are returning, everything is very fluid, as an observer it's interesting watch, but the implications of what's happening will have far reaching consequences for the masses. So much for the state of the nation here as GB sees it. On a more personal note, I survive from day to day, have become more insular, not really motivated to do anything. I blame it on age, one gets to 45 and is not quite sure about what to do in the future. I am seriously thinking of returning to Jamaica at the end of next year i.e. early 1986. But as normal I don't want to think so far ahead. So much can happen in another year. We might have a world revolution.[47]

While she was not able to involve herself in political work in Zimbabwe, she remained active in Black British politics from a distance. Toward the tail end of its life as a project, OWAAD had been approached by the publisher Virago to write an account of Black women's lives in Britain. As a result, leading members of the movement, including Gerlin, Beverley Bryan, Stella Dadzie and Suzanne Scafe, took up this task to write what would become the seminal book on the topic of Black women in Britain, *Heart of the Race*. Due to Gerlin's move to Zimbabwe she was not able to participate fully in the writing process as she had planned since this required intensive research and oral history interviewing as well as co-writing, which were not possible from such a distance. However, she insisted on being kept up to date on the progress of the book, and also provided ideas on its content. In particular, she was excited by what became the fourth chapter: 'Chain Reactions: Black Women Organising'.[48] Although it is difficult to discern the degree to which her suggestions shaped the book, they are reminders of her political outlook, which was synonymous with the Black Women's Movement's theorisations from the pages of *Speak Out*, *FOWAAD*, and the speeches of the first National Black Women's Conference. Her suggestions also exhibit an appreciation of the wider history of

Black women's political organising in Britain, which was a fundamental element of politicisation for Black women activists. Her
name appears in the list of acknowledgements to all the women
who had contributed their stories, or support to the project. The
following suggestions appear in a letter she wrote to Stella dated 27
July 1987:

Organisation and Resistance

To locate the nature of our resistance in Britain. Perhaps
you might want to mention – a little of the history of our
resistance in the Caribbean especially pre-Independence. The
women were fundamental in organising inside the political
parties, rallies, demonstrations, in trade unions – there is
some documentation, but not only as usual our struggles have
been omitted, or just documented as part and parcel of the
whole Black resistance – I feel this point needs to be made.
Because although we have played crucial roles in all the Black
struggles – famous men have been mentioned but not women.
So whatever the struggle is about, we know that women have
participated and have been the backbone of these struggles.

- For e.g. the "Notting Hill Gate riots" I wasn't around
  at that time, but I was told that women were there side
  by side fighting physically, against those white racists.
  I know no one who you could talk to about this – Gus
  John in his book 'Because we are Black' might have
  written something I can't remember.
- There is lots about the 'Brixton uprising', can't be left
  out.
- 1972 Auxiliaries and SEN's hospital strike.
- 1974 Nurse's strike – Black women were instrumental
  in these
- Most of these struggles can be attributed to the women
  who came in the '50s and '60s.
- Must also point out that the 2nd generation Black
  woman has carried on this tradition of struggle. E.g.
  on confrontation with police – if you take Olive Morris

and the Nigerian diplomat. Also it is here all the
1981/82 uprisings could fit in
- Confrontation with authorities – "rebellion of survival"
  against the State e.g. Social security, social service –
  educational authorities.

Sorry I am unable to formulate these things in any coherent
fashion, but I need to see the outline again of that chapter.
See I haven't got any of the relevant material, and seen it so
late in the day. These are just reminders, I am sure it's all
there already. As it's difficult to interview myself, I can't even
give you that benefit. As I was thinking about this chapter, it
could be one of the most exciting chapters of the book.

The old Race Todays, all the old organisational papers, this
is the only place where I think IRR could be used for their
materials, because whatever the resistance was we were there.
All this history we are writing whilst we are still living it, so
it's difficult to see. But somehow it has to come across in the
chapters as somehow I wish I was there to participate in the
discussions on this chapter.[49]

Gerlin's decision to remain in Zimbabwe longer than the initial two
years of her contract seemed to have less to do with her inclination
to prolong working there and more to do with her disillusionment
with Britain. During her time in Zimbabwe she frequently considered where she would end up next. In July 1984 she was already
considering returning to Jamaica, but was also open to the possibility of moving to Ghana.[50] In a letter a year later, in May 1985,
she reaffirmed her commitment not to move back to Britain, while
also contemplating Zimbabwe's first five years of independence: '5
years is still a short time and some progress has been made. I am
sure it'd still be as depressing and awful as Britain. I have really
decided I couldn't live there any longer. So I am seriously going
to check JA out in July'.[51] During her third year in Zimbabwe she
began making concrete plans for her repatriation to Jamaica, and
again illustrated her low emotional state in Zimbabwe, due in large
part to her political isolation:

I am now looking forward to finish my contract this year and to move on, to what I don't know, and perhaps Reagan and Thatcher might have blown up the world or started the 3rd world war. Zimbabwe is a very nice place to live in if you are not Zimbabwean and [are] marginal to everything. For people like me, it's soul destroying, because there isn't much I can get involved in, there is no stimulation. As I don't want to live in England anymore I have decided Jamaica is the only other place to go. So by next year June I shall be there.

I am not quite sure how you sisters are coping in the UK. Things seem to be also at a stand still with each individual doing his or her own thing. Now with the demise of the GLC what will happen to all the projects which were started by it, and all the workers.[52]

RETURNING TO JAMAICA

Before moving back to Jamaica Gerlin stopped briefly in London, where she found herself quickly in demand by the Black radical movement. She recalled a period where, having not left her house for days, the phone rang with a request for her presence at a meeting to help settle an argument between activists. Gerlin's daughter answered the phone and made up an excuse so Gerlin could stay at home undetected.[53] Her dependability and status as a leader in the Black movement led her to suffer exhaustion, and it is likely that this, along with the increasingly hostile political environment in Britain, which encouraged her swift move to Jamaica in the spring of 1987. Writing to Stella in April after recently arriving to Jamaica, Gerlin described her low mental state in London during a stop off visit: 'Returning to the wet and cold of London knowing that I have left Zimbabwe threw me into a right dep … So I didn't feel like seeing anyone'.[54] Eighteen years after her move back to Jamaica, Gerlin recalled that the underlying reason for leaving London behind was because she no longer felt a sense of belonging: 'After Zimbabwe I decided I couldn't go back to England to live so I was just coming straight home, and I did come straight home. Why? I just felt detached. Although my daughter and the grandchildren were there, I didn't feel a part anymore'.[55] Returning to Jamaica had the desired effect on her mood. As always, she was eager to scope out the activist scene, writing again in August that 'it's nice being home, should have returned ages ago, better late than never. I am trying hard to re-orientate myself to the environment and society as a whole. This period is very important in making contacts, sussing out the various tendencies and personalities. There is a lot to learn and will take a long time understanding how things really function. However, I am also trying to have fun, enjoying the sea and sun, the beautiful places that I didn't see as a child'.[56]

FINDING COMMUNITY

It didn't take long for Gerlin to 'reorient' herself in Jamaica and become involved in local activities. It proved a fairly easy task to make connections, especially with other returnees. One such connection was with Nzingha Assata, who had also recently moved back to Jamaica with her children from southwest London. Nzingha, like Gerlin, was involved in Black community work in London. Having initially participated in the Black Unity and Freedom Party (BUFP) from 1984 to 1985, Nzingha found herself more aligned to culturally nationalist and Pan-Africanist projects. She was a founding member of Harriet Tubman Sisters, a Black women's group established in 1985, and also participated in Headstart bookshop and supplementary school.[57] While both Nzingha and Gerlin were active in Black community organising in London, they were active in different years and thus hadn't encountered each other until their move back to Jamaica, as Nzingha explained:

> I decided to go to Jamaica, I decided to take my children out of school for a year … we rented a house and lived there and that was how I met Gerlin because I also attended the Marcus Garvey centenary conference at the University of the West Indies in Kingston. And me and Gerlin hit it off that day and we hung around. So, October 1987 I met Gerlin … she wasn't sure if she was staying, she was going to go back to Zimbabwe … after the conference, we didn't have contact

again. And then in March of 1988, I attended International
Women's Day in Kingston, and there was Gerlin.[58]

It was through Nzingha that Gerlin found a job with 3D Projects,
which she remained committed to developing for the rest of her
working life. 3D Projects was Jamaica's first fully established
community-based rehabilitation programme, supporting disabled
youth and their families.[59] Nzingha recalled how Gerlin began to
settle in Jamaica with her new job and home:

I was working on a project in Spanish Town called 3D
Projects, dedicated to the development of the disabled. And
I was the coordinator for the workers who went into the
homes, teaching parents how to stimulate disabled children.
So Gerlin was looking for somewhere to live, and also a job
because she had applied to the Ministry of Health, etc. And
nothing was forthcoming. So because I was only staying in
the job until June, I took her details. And she took my details.
And I said, 'I'll speak to the manager and see what they've
got to say'. And so I spoke to the manager, and they had two
jobs. One was for a training coordinator … that was the one
that Gerlin came and got at 3D Projects in Spanish Town, 14
Monk Street, St. Catherine. And so we've kept in touch ever
since then, because she moved around the corner to where I
had rented a house in a place called Meadowvale, in Portmore
of Jamaica. And there was another place called Gregory Park
where Gerlin got a small flat to rent. So we were literally, if
you like, in close proximity to each other.[60]

Gerlin and Nzingha worked together on a number of community
projects geared towards celebrating and promoting Black history,
culture and liberation politics. They used to attend events that were
organised by the University of the West Indies, such as celebrations for Nelson Mandela's release. In addition, alongside another
activist and Garveyite Beverley Hamilton, Gerlin and Nzingha
worked as part of a committee to organise annual Africa Liberation
Day celebrations.[61] According to Nzingha, Beverley had already
been working on projects such as this prior to them meeting her,

'so Gerlin and I kind of joined up with that'.[62] In addition to this work around events, Gerlin and others including Cecil Gutzmore produced *Echo,* which, like the publications they had worked on in London, served as an alternative Black political newspaper.[63] The newspaper took an anti-colonial and Pan-Africanist line; for example, in its May 1994 issue the editorial included a critique of the granting of Jamaican independence and the decolonisation process: 'Independence was handed down to us in 1962 without allowing us to develop and create our own systems that would enhance our progress ... A colonised people need a complete break from their colonisers in order to develop their own new systems to suit their needs'.[64] Issues included topics such as the Black Family, international affairs, opinion pieces, youth, disabilities, lifestyle, and more. The coverage of disabilities and youth was likely part of Gerlin's remit as part of the Echo collective.

3D PROJECTS AND HEALTH ADVOCACY

Beginning as a training coordinator, Gerlin climbed the ranks of 3D Projects over the years to become the organisation's managing director in 2002. 3D Projects was a pioneering initiative in Jamaica, where disabilities were still poorly understood and a neglected topic. Support services in the St Catherine parish where she was based were non-existent. In connection with her work on supporting disabled youth, she also obtained a Master's degree in public health.[65] Her work at 3D was not only focused on coordinating support services for disabled youth and their families, but also raising awareness around disabled children and challenging harmful misconceptions about the causes of disabilities, and ableism more generally. With this, she became a leading voice on the topic of disability rights in Jamaica. In 1995 Gerlin co-wrote a paper with Marigold J. Thorburn on the importance of mobilising parents in the fight for proper services for disabled youth:

In many countries around the world, services for children and adults with developmental disabilities have come about because of the efforts of parents. In Europe much of this began in the 1930s. In this, as in many other respects, developing countries have lagged behind. This may be partly because a larger segment of their population has been disadvantaged in other ways which put disability as a low priority. There is more poverty, services of all kinds are fewer and they are less accessible ... Consequently advocacy efforts are stifled. There is probably more ignorance and shame about disability because the population at large have not been exposed to relevant and accurate information. Nor are they aware of the newer trends particularly those relating to rights of persons with disabilities.[66]

Gerlin organised workshops in the community to tackle these issues around misinformation. One such workshop was held in St Mary, one of Jamaica's smallest parishes, in February 1994, and was reported in the *Kingston Gleaner*: 'Citizens of St Mary and its environs will have the opportunity to learn more about the types and causes of various disabilities ... There are many myths and misconceptions surrounding disability and the disabled'.[67] Gerlin was quoted as stating that: 'one can become disabled by any number of factors. Problems can occur as early as conception, or at birth and there are accidents or illnesses which can occur at any age, to any one of us'.[68] As the demands and scope of 3D Projects continued to grow, it became increasingly important to source funds. In 1999 the Jamaica Social Investment Fund provided $2.36 million to the Project for a work experience programme for its young people. Gerlin explained that the programme had been running since as early as 1992.[69] Despite this cash injection, 3D Projects struggled to obtain the finances needed to continue, especially as the service was in such high demand from the community. In 2002 Gerlin wrote an urgent appeal for public support, explaining that prior overseas funding from donors had stopped, and that the government was not able to match the prior level of funding: 'If we cut back any further then we may as well close down the organisation. This would be a pity as 3D Projects has had many successes, and is one of the leading organisations on disability issues in the region'.[70] This highlights the constant struggle of such services which, though essential, were often in precarious financial situations as care providers.[71] The situation remained the same in 2009, as Gerlin listed the challenges of her work: 'we don't have any money, we have to do fundraising or we have to write a lot of proposals ... and the demands are great, we don't have the skills in the organisation because we're so low paid. And you can't get the people with the proficiency to carry out certain activities, and so many of the people who we train are parents'.[72] This was reflected in the 2002 appeal, which detailed the staff of 3D Projects. The appeal suggests that the Project at that time was women and parent-led: 'services are carried out by a team of 60 dedicated, well-trained women many of whom are mothers of children with disabilities'.[73] 3D Projects was a continuation of Gerlin's long career history of supporting marginalised people and communities, and providing them with the tools to improve their conditions. As she explained: 'anything I do is about transference of skills to the local people. I work with children with disabilities but we train people to be rehabilitation workers. And they go into homes and they work with the parents – how to manage the child, whatever kind of disability it is. And they are trained to transfer their skills to the family members'.[74] 3D Projects had a widespread impact, not only on the children who were cared for and nurtured by it, but also their parents. As Gerlin attested to, women were particularly affected by the demand to care for their disabled child when there was no external support service available. In many instances the mother was abandoned by the father due to misunderstandings and prejudices around disability, and the mother was therefore cut off from any opportunity of furthering her own education or career, which could in some cases lead to resentment and neglect of the child. To relieve the care burden on these women, in addition to the home visits that the 3D Projects provided Gerlin and the team worked hard to fundraise for a day centre:

> Some of the parents are young parents, a young woman have her first child ... she can't go to school to finish her education, she can't go to work she has no one to care for them because the man has gone, the moment it's a disability, 'it's not mine'. What happens is that the woman has to care for this child with not many services, and she doesn't want to put the child

into one of these homes, it's her child, it's her close child she
loves that child regardless ... but its [sic] hard in Jamaica, it's
hard for her, she can't run, so when we intervene we don't
have a home for children, we go into the homes and we work
with you, and we try to assist you and tell you what to do and
what to help the child ... it's hard, so what I'm trying to do
and I'm telling them is to minimise any kind of child abuse in
that situation or whatever. If we have a place, so we can work
with the children. The mother can go to school, go wherever,
and do whatever she wants, but she doesn't have the child 24
hours per day. So many people can't see that that makes sense
because we're working in a really deprived community, and a
volatile area and stuff like that, but it will work.

Eventually, this goal came to fruition. In June 2009, with
$717,000 raised by the local Spanish Town community, and the
help of a Jamaica Social Investment Fund in restoring a building,
the 3D Early Childhood Centre for Children with Disabilities
was unveiled on Monk Street. It opened officially in September
of that year.[75] At the time of its opening, the Centre could accom-
modate up to fifty children between the ages of three and six,
and catered to children with neurodiversity and learning difficulties as well as physical disabilities. By 2009 Gerlin had dedicated
twenty-two years to developing the 3D Projects, ensuring its
survival, and expanding its services. Now in her advanced years,
she aimed to carry the Project to a place of safety and sustain-
ability before retiring, stating: 'being the Managing Director is
hard work and if I knew it was going to be so rough, I would have
said, "No thank you!" I want to go to the beach and be "under-
resourced". I am really trying to bring it back, to get resources
to bring it to a certain standard, and then I will bow out'.[76] 3D
Projects is still operational under a new name – Community Based
Rehabilitation Jamaica (CBRJ) – a testament to Gerlin's enduring
commitment to the work. Alongside this, Gerlin also held the
position of Board Chairman of Children First Jamaica from its
inception in 1997. Children First Jamaica operates out of 9 Monk
Street in Spanish Town, a few doors away from CBRJ. Its services
include its Youth Wellness Center, which works to equip young

people with the education and healthcare skills needed to reduce the risk of contracting HIV, as well as educational and vocational skills training and job placements; and Project GYAL, descrived as an 'advocacy, literacy and empowerment campaign aimed at reducing Gender Based Violence in Jamaica'.[77] In 2020, Children First awarded Gerlin a tribute, recognising her twenty-three years of service and describing her contributions as follows:

> With her keen eye for detail and her hands-on approach, Ms Bean was actively involved in the daily operations of the Agency, always lending a helping hand where and when she could. Her drive and passion have definitely made her a force to reckon with when it comes to positively influencing young minds. What can we learn from our Board Chairman? Be passionate about anything that you do in life; Let yourself become submerged in it and hold nothing back.[78]

NOTES

1 Gerlin Bean, letter to Stella Dadzie, 14 February 1983.
2 A. Sivanandan, 'RAT and the degradation of Black Struggle', *Race & Class*, Vol 15, 1983, pp1-11.
3 Alongside Sivanandan's work, see a useful discussion on this shift toward neoliberalism in Camilla Schofield, Florence Sutcliffe-Braithwaite and Rob Waters, '"The privatisation of the struggle": an anti-racism in the age of enterprise', in Aled Davies, Ben Jackson, and Florence Sutcliffe-Braithwaite (eds), *The Neoliberal Age? Britain Since the 1970s*, UCL Press: London, 2021, pp206-213.
4 Alex Scott-Samuel, Clare Bambra, Chik Collins, David J. Hunter, Gerry McCartney and Kat Smith, 'The Impact of Thatcherism on Health and Well-being in Britain', *International Journal of Health Studies*, Vol 44, No 1, 2014, p54.
5 Karibu Education Centre, www.karibueducationcentre.org.uk/.
6 Milo Miller (ed), *Speak Out!: The Brixton Black Women's Group,* Verso: London, 2023.
7 Gerlin Bean, 'No, We Didn't Burn Our Bras', in Hilary Robertson-Hickling (ed), *That Time in Foreign*, Hansib, 2016, p157.
8 Aaron Rwodzi, 'Reconciliation: a False Start in Zimbabwe? (1980-1990)', *Cogent Arts and Humanities*, Vol 7, No 1, 2020.
9 Barbara Ward, 20 October 1980, in Michael Walsh, *From Sword to*

Ploughshare: Sword of the Spirit to Catholic Institute of International Relations 1940-1980, CIIR: London, 1980, p4.

10 Ibid.

11 Jon Barnes, *A Record of Change in a Changing World*, Progressio: London, 2019, p359.

12 Gerlin Bean, 'Heart of the Race: Oral Histories of the Black Women's Movement', Black Cultural Archives: ORAL/1/3, 2009, p18; hereafter BCA.

13 Bean 2016, op cit, p158.

14 Ibid.

15 Bean 2009, op cit, p18.

16 Hugh MacCamley interviewed by the author, 1 March 2023.

17 Bean 2016, op cit, p159.

18 MacCamley, op cit.

19 Bean 2016, op cit, pp157-158.

20 Ibid.

21 Gerlin Bean, letter to Stella Dadzie, 14 November 1983.

22 Chimurenga is a Shona word which means revolutionary struggle or uprising. The Ndebele equivalent word is Umvukela.

23 Eliakim M. Sibanda, *The Zimbabwe African People's Union 1961-87: A Political History of Insurgency in Southern Rhodesia*, Africa World Press: Trenton and Asmara, 2005, p2.

24 Edson Zvobgo, 'Oppression of Women is Dead,' *The Chronicle*, 22 May 1980.

25 Thokozile Ushe, 'Girl's Role in the Struggle', *The Zimbabwe Review*, Vol 6, No 10, October 1977, p1.

26 Robert Mugabe, 'Message to the World Conference of the United Nations Decade for Women', delivered by Sally Mugabe, Copenhagen, July 1980.

27 Kate Law, '"We Wanted to be free as a nation, and we wanted to be free as women": Decolonisation, Nationalism and Women's Liberation in Zimbabwe, 1979-85', *Gender & History*, Vol 33, No 1, 2021, pp249-268.

28 Tanya Lyons, 'Guerrilla Girls and Women in the Zimbabwean Liberation Struggle', in Jean Allman, Susan Geiger and Nakanyike Musisi (eds), *Women in African Colonial Histories*, 2002, p306.

29 For examples elsewhere on the African continent, see Stephanie Urdang, 'Fighting Two Colonialisms: The Women's Struggle in Guinea-Bissau', *African Studies Review*, Vol 18, No 3, December 1975, pp29-34.

30 At the time of writing, Gerlin's letters are planned to be deposited at the Black Cultural Archives within Stella Dadzie's existing collection.

31 Gerlin Bean, letter to Stella Dadzie, 14 February 1983.
32 Gerlin Bean, letter to Stella Dadzie, 19 April 1983.
33 For more information, see William J. Mpofu, 'Gukurahundi in Zimbabwe: An Epistemicide and Genocide', *Journal of Literary Studies*, Vol 37, No 2, 2021, pp40-55.
34 Gerlin Bean, letter to Stella Dadzie, 19 April 1983.
35 See Law, op cit, pp249-268; Gay W. Seidman, 'Women in Zimbabwe: Post-Independence Struggles', *Feminist Studies*, Vol 10, No 3, Autumn 1984, pp419-440; and Patricia Chogugudza, 'Gender and War: Zimbabwean Women and the Liberation Struggle', *War and Society*, January 2006.
36 Law, op cit, p253.
37 Bean April 1983, op cit.
38 Ibid.
39 Gerlin Bean, letter to Stella Dadzie, 30 August 1983.
40 Gerlin Bean, letter to Stella Dadzie, 14 November 1983.
41 Seidman, op cit, pp419-440.
42 Ibid.
43 Law, op cit, pp253.
44 Bean November 1983, op cit.
45 Ibid.
46 Ibid.
47 Gerlin Bean, letter to Stella Dadzie, 17 October 1984.
48 Bryan et al, op cit, *Heart of the Race: Black Women's Lives in Britain*, Virago: London, 1985, pp124-181.
49 Gerlin Bean, letter to Stella Dadzie, 27 July 1987.
50 Gerlin Bean, letter to Stella Dadze, 27 July 1984.
51 Gerlin Bean, letter to Stella Dadzie, 11 May 1985.
52 Gerlin Bean, letter to Stella Dadzie, 20 April 1986.
53 Gerlin Bean in conversation with the author at BCA, 28 June 2018.
54 Gerlin Bean, letter to Stella Dadzie, 26 April 1987
55 Bean 2016, op cit, p160.
56 Gerlin Bean, letter to Stella Dadzie, 11 August 1987.
57 Minutes from Harriet Tubman Sisters meeting, 27 July 1985, BCA: ASSATA/1/5. See also Nzingha Assata interviewed by the author, 10 September 2022, p4.
58 Assata, op cit.
59 Community Based Rehabilitation Jamaica, www.cbrj.org/.
60 Assata, op cit.
61 Africa Liberation Day committee meeting minutes, 12 April 1988, BCA: ASSATA/2/3.
62 Assata, op cit.

63 Assata, op cit.

64 'Editorial: Changes', *Echo: The Family Newspaper*, No 2, May 1994, p2.

65 Gerlin Bean and Marigold J. Thorburn, 'Mobilising Parents of Children with Disabilities in Jamaica and the English Speaking Caribbean', in Bryan O'Toole and Roy McConkey (eds), *Innovations in Developing Countries for People with Disabilities*, Lisieux Hall Publications: Chorley, 1995, p107.

66 Ibid, p94.

67 'St. Mary orientation on disability', *Kingston Gleaner*, 20 February 1994.

68 Ibid.

69 'JSIF backs the disabled', *Kingston Gleaner*, 27 May 1999.

70 'An Urgent Appeal: Become a friend of 3D Projects', *Kingston Gleaner*, 15 April 2002.

71 M.J. Thorburn. 'A Community Approach to Helping Disabled Children in Jamaica', *International Journal of Mental Health*, Vol 20, No 2, Summer, 1990, pp61-75.

72 Bean 2009, op cit, pp19-20.

73 Ibid.

74 Ibid, p19.

75 Robert Turner, 'New School for Ja's Challenged', *Kingston Gleaner*, 29 June 2009.

76 Bean 2016, op cit, p160.

77 Children First Agency, 'Our Projects', www.childrenfirstja.org/projects-initiatives.

78 Children First Jamaica, 'In appreciation of your 23 years of service', www.facebook.com, 23 July 2020.

7

Legacy

Due to Gerlin's deteriorating health, she moved back to London from Jamaica to receive care in 2020. As I mentioned in the introduction, it had been my initial hope for Gerlin to be much more involved in this biography, in order to tell her life story in her own words. However, memories of Gerlin from those who knew her have provided the glue to piecing together what began as fragmented pieces of a rich activist life. Such recollections have formed a significant part of this work and have performed a great service to the preservation of Gerlin's legacy. It is only fitting that we close this book in the same vein. This space is therefore dedicated to presenting tributes to Gerlin Bean from her close friends and comrades. Undoubtedly, the below testimonies about her commitment to causes for social justice, and the connections she has made throughout her life, are just the tip of the iceberg. They provide us with an insight into the immense impact she has had on others throughout her lifetime, and I hope will preserve her legacy for generations to come. It is also my hope that these testimonies might motivate others to similarly share their recollections of Gerlin, to aid in the recovery process. This book is only the beginning; a digital space has been created entitled The Gerlin Bean Project where resources and information related to Gerlin, as they continue to be produced, will be made easily accessible. My hope is that this digital space will continue to foster interest in Gerlin's history as an example of lifelong commitment to radical politics, Black liberation, Black women's empowerment, community building, and solidarity across struggles. If you have a story to share, please do get in touch at gerlinbeanproject.com. History-writing, much like history-making, is a collective task, after all.

Zainab Abbas

Former International Secretary of the Black Liberation Front and founding member of the Brixton Black Women's Group

Gerlin and I have been close friends for over fifty years. When I first met her at the Gresham Project, I was in my early twenties, and she her early thirties. The eleven-year age difference between us meant that she was a mentor to myself and other young black radicals in Brixton. At the time I was squatting a house on Railton Road with Olive Morris and Liz Obi. The Panthers, then led by Darcus Howe, would often meet in our house. Gerlin was then, and remained for the rest of her conscious life, a feminist. She was particularly concerned about how sisters, who were in the forefront of the Black movement, were often sidelined and not given credit for their ideas and revolutionary practices.

She persuaded myself, Olive and Liz to meet at Marcia's place, a young sister with a small child who would find it hard to meet at other venues. That first meeting was exciting and filled with laughter as we contemplated the behaviour of brothers in our various organisations. Gerlin and I were Black Liberation Front Members and Olive and Liz were Brixton Panthers. Most of that first meeting was taken up with hilarious examples of misogynist behaviour from our male comrades to the point we were all belly laughing. However, we all understood the meeting could be a catalyst for a defined feminist agenda. Many meetings later, we were joined by more sisters from the BLF, the Brixton Panthers and the BUFP. Our ideological differences were very much in the forefront when the Barbara Beese and Leila Hassan wanted to discuss a theoretical concept from Selma James called 'Wages for Housework'.

Selma James was not a member or even a supporter of the Brixton Black Women's Group but her ideas managed to cause an enormous split in what had then become an Organisation. Gerlin fought tooth and nail to keep us on track discussing feminism, but cracks had already begun to appear. Fifty-odd years on, I find it difficult to bear that others claim credit for founding the Brixton Black Women's Group. It did not emanate from the Panthers nor the BLF; it emanated from a group of sisters brought together by our most prominent feminist at the time, Gerlin Bean. Finally, Gerlin spent her life dedicated to the Black community, whether in Britain, Zimbabwe or Jamaica. Her love for her people is inspirational and her support and championing of young people in particular helped put many youth on the right track to survive the all-pervading culture of racism. She is an unsung hero that should take her place in our history books

Nzingha Assata
Pan-Afrikanist, historian and writer

I have known Gerlin for many, many, years, having met her in October 1987 at the Marcus Garvey Centenary conference held at the University of the West Indies (UWI) in Kingston Jamaica. Gerlin is a great friend, her kindness is unending, she is empathetic and a great support to her family, friends and to her people.

Gerlin can be considered to be one of a kind, an asset to the Black community and to the world at large. She has shown a strong ability to critique and analyse oppressive forces that seek to exploit others less able to stand up for themselves and in this regard, she will mobilise with others to stand up for the human rights of others. She can be described as an anti-colonial, anti-imperialist champion.

As an agent for change she has always been willing to step forward to play an active role in providing services for people across all sections of society; for youths; the disabled; women and for her people as a whole. She shared her extensive resources of books, money, her knowledge and her time and she is one who is never seeking to make a name for herself or seeking financial reward.

I have worked with Gerlin, mostly in Jamaica, where we would organise events in the community with sister Beverley Hamilton, a Garveyite. We would organise events such as Afrika Liberation Day (ALD); Marcus Garvey Birthday celebrations; exhibitions for Black History Month and more. Gerlin is a great speaker, presenter and someone who means what she says and stands by her word. A real

Afrikan warrior Queen. The children and staff at 3D Projects in Jamaica always valued Gerlin and reacted with joy when she arrived at work or if they came across her in the street.

As people of Afrikan heritage, we need to make sure that contributors to our story such as Gerlin are valued, celebrated, acknowledged and remembered for their dedicated service.

Stella Dadzie

Founding member of the Organisation of Women of Asian and African Descent, historian and writer

I have known Gerlin since the mid 1970s, and love her dearly. More than a close friend, she was also a political mentor, and not just to me. It was her sense of community, her opposition to injustice, and her consistent example that inspired many women to get involved in Brixton BWG. She understood the way race, gender and class impacted on our lives and had a clear, consistent analysis of where our priorities lay. Her influence was equally central to the way OWAAD evolved. Perhaps because she was a little older than most of us, many women regarded her as a mother-figure – someone to turn to for comfort and advice. If anyone deserves the title 'grand-mother of black feminism', it is her. When she left for Zimbabwe in the early 80s, she left a Gerlin-shaped hole in countless lives.

We were always close, but our friendship grew stronger in the aftermath of Olive Morris's death in July 1979. We needed to get away, and decided to travel to America together. We bought two, cheap, standby tickets to Chicago, where we stayed with a friend who lived on South Side, the so-called 'armpit of America'. I'll always remember our friend's advice. She took one look at the two of us with our free and easy, London-black-girl ways and reminded us we weren't in Brixton now. 'Never go out with more than $10 in your purse,' she said. 'Wear your aint-got-shit clothes. And don't go talking with any brothers who look like they don't have a job.'

Gerlin, who was used to feeling safe and grounded in her community, wasn't inclined to heed the advice. Everyone knew her in Brixton, including the jobless youths on Railton Road. She felt as at home on South Side Chicago as she did backyard. Years later, when I visited her in Spanish Town, things were no different. I walked the streets untroubled because local people knew I was staying with Miss Bean, whose advocacy and support for disabled people and their families had earned the community's respect.

While in Chicago we met with some sisters from the National Alliance of Black Women and took part in some of their discussions. We then took a Greyhound – 'the dawg' as it was known – from the East to the West Coast to visit my convalescent father, who had recently suffered a stroke. We walked barefoot on the beaches of San Diego, travelled to Mexico, took a lift from a brother in LA who turned out to be a raving misogynist. We refer to this time as our Thelma & Louise trip because we spent a night in his home, up in the hills, convinced we were going to be murdered. Fortunately, we came out of it unscathed, but we have often talked about that night when we sat back to back on the bed, ready to fight for our lives, and how differently things might have turned out.

When Gerlin left Zimbabwe in the mid 1980s, she moved to Jamaica. I still have her letters in which she explained her reasons for leaving and her decision not to return to London. I have visited her several times over the years, and we have always stayed close. We slip into our friendship like we were never apart. I am so glad someone has recognised the need to pay tribute to Gerlin. In the struggle for Black civil rights in this country, she stood head and shoulders above many of the men whose names are remembered. It's high time her significance to that struggle, and to the Black woman's movement in particular, was fully acknowledged.

Beverley Bryan

Former member of the Black Panther Movement, founding member of Brixton Black Women's Group and Organisation of Women of Asian and African Descent, Professor of Language Education

I'd worked with Gerlin for more than ten years before she moved to Zimbabwe. We had set up the Brixton Black Women's group together and had really laboured to keep the group together. Even though we had no formal leaders in BWG, Gerlin was one of the women I most looked to for support and encouragement. She was someone you could totally rely on. I think she offered a lot of support to many different women in the group.

It was some time after the Black Women's Centre was established that Gerlin decided she was going to work in Zimbabwe. We did talk about it. I think she felt that with the number of women's group expanding and the Centre open that at this time a stage had been reached for her to do something else. She had a strong internationalist perspective from our group's contacts with women from the African liberation struggles: Eritrea, Namibia, Zimbabwe, South Africa, Mozambique etc.

Gerlin had good health and health management experience that she was not using as much as she could. She had also completed an applied social science degree at the London School of Economics (LSE). She wanted to put that knowledge and those skills to good use in a newly liberated country that needed her support. And Zimbabwe was a good choice: we were rooting for them. The social fabric of the society was in disarray with the war and the apartheid conditions of white minority rule. Additionally, many fighters had come back from the liberation war as paraplegics who needed to be introduced to a new way of living. The work was urgent and volunteers were needed.

Gerlin's leaving was a blow to us, certainly to me. After I knew she was settled there, a few years later, I decided to go and visit her with my two young sons of five and eight years old.

It was an enlightening and inspiring experience. First, I could reconnect with a number of Zimbabweans we had known as part of the wider liberation movement, who had been based in London. These were women and men who were now decision makers – in the Ministry of Health, Culture, Women's Affairs, etc. It was heady at that time to see those comrades now in the position of governing. At that time the optimism was still high. The fighting had not concluded and there were security concerns because Nkomo's troops were still active. So it really felt as though you were witnessing a sister working at the forefront to help build a new country

I could see the important work that Gerlin was doing. Part of her work was to encourage nurses and doctors to join her in helping Zimbabwe get back on its feet as a newly independent Black country. I was personally surprised to reconnect with the obstetrician who had delivered my youngest son in London's St Thomas' Hospital in Harare; she was at least a hospital resident so I knew that Gerlin was persuasive in getting the best!

Gerlin worked with NGOs but liaised most closely with the Ministry of Health. Part of that work, too, was supporting and empowering women to help them build their families, communities and country through bodily autonomy, self-sufficiency and entrepreneurship. So, connecting with these different ministries was important as well as getting to know the networks operating across the country. It was inspiring to see that work, especially as it was all so new and pioneering.

We visited different parts of the country: I remember travelling to eastern Matabeleland, Victoria Falls in the North West on the border with Zambia, and the region of the Great Zimbabwe in the south and right down to the border with South Africa, even while that country was still under apartheid. Although I did not visit the latter country, I know Gerlin did because, of course, the network of activists extended there also. In each region I could see the work that was being done in Zimbabwe and how Gerlin was contributing. As I was working in education, I felt inspired myself by the positive impact of it and seriously thought of joining her in that work.

Gail Lewis

Former member of the Brixton Black Women's Group, Organisation of Women of Asian and African Descent, psychotherapist and researcher

Gerlin, she was a major figure in Brixton. I suppose I want to say two things really. One, she modelled the way of being a pivot that connected up all sorts of different separate organisations. She was really a pivot in that sense. Probably exhausting herself in stuff. But, it's that thing about at local level, replicating the idea that we need to link any individual struggle together. That, and she also modelled inside the group – I don't know what she'd feel if she heard me say this – how to do leadership that was about collective thinking and decision making and action, even though she was a leader. She did help us to think what the strategic goals should be, and tactically how we might get there ... What I mean by leader in that sense, there was a clarity of things. And it was also, as a leadership thing, enabling us to own our own responsibility and our own capacities that fed into the collective project. So she kind of let us uncurl from ourselves, so she could really do that. And she could draw people together, because she can speak to every-body, people were drawn to her. Don't get me wrong, she could tell you off. Or she could get vexed about stuff. I don't mean timidness. But I mean, a capacity for really attending to what's going on, and thinking about how we might move from there and calculate our capacity to do that in our own ways. That, for me, is what a leader is.

Ansel Wong

Former member of the Black Liberation Front, Principle of Ahfiwe and Gresham Project youth worker, cultural activist

For two decades Brixton was the cultural, political and social front line of the Black community – an epicentre that I entered in the 1970s, straight out of university and into my first job at Sydenham Girls School in Forest Hill. Brixton had its attractions for the Caribbean diaspora: the market with recognisable products, the celebrated pub and the jumping off point for the whole of South London. Workers like me were attracted here. It is here that I first met Gerlin. The Gresham Project, a youth club that had the unique distinction to be sited obliquely opposite the Brixton Police Station, in full view and within earshot of the cries of prisoners in deten-tion in the cells. Gresham, the Police Station and bus stops outside Woolworths were intersections that we crisscrossed in our work. This is the seventies with the moral panics over mugging, Sus and the SPG – the elite Police Squad that targeted the Black commu-nity in Brixton.

   Gerlin was at the heart of the resistance to these incursions into our community. She pioneered our responses, brought us together and drove the agenda for change and interventions. Two incidents epitomised this, working with the youths in the area – in fact, from the whole of South London down to Thornton Heath. At the time, there was just one main bus stop outside Woolworths and everyone had to congregate there, striving to board the many buses – a very attractive flow of people for the dipping and picking of pockets. That was Gerlin's hot spot. She patrolled that area engaging with the youths, knowing full well that no action would take place in her presence, such was the respect they had for her. What illustrated this for me was to see two youths go up to her and enquire which bus she was waiting for. On telling them that she was just 'waiting', one of the youths remarked, 'Please, miss, you spoiling it for us. We can't work with you here'.

Gerlin intervened in the lives of many young people in Lambeth, developing strong bonds and being an inspirational matriarch, confidante and source of information, especially young girls. My second moment of her seminal interventions was a visit to the West End to outreach to teenage girls truanting from schools in Lambeth. I accompanied her on one of these trips. It was not difficult identifying girls we knew from Brixton. Again, with deference to Gerlin, they agreed to talk to us. Off we went to a Wimpy. It was brilliant to see her at work, engaging, empathising and being able to answer their every justification for what they were doing in the West End. The defining moment came when one of the girls pulled out a wad of notes and told us that this is what she earned in two hours. 'Miss, you asking me to go back to school. To get a CSE and to work in Woolworths? Ah not getting this in Woolworths'. Gerlin did not give up on those girls. She maintained a relationship that lasted several years and it was a joy to have encountered them several years later and have them acknowledge the importance of her intervention in their lives. Gerlin Bean – Mother, matriarch, MaComère.

Neveta Johnson-Fuller

Former 3D Projects worker

I am feeling so elated to be asked to share my memoirs about Gerlin Bean. When Dr McFarlane called and asked, I felt butterflies in my stomach ... I did shed some tears, I wanted to write everything but I know that time wasn't available. I first met Ms Bean on Monday, 2 December 1991 at 3D Projects at 14 Monk Street, Spanish Town, St Catherine, Jamaica. She was the Deputy Director and was one of the panellists scheduled to do my interview. Did I tell you? This was the start of a beautiful journey. I was hired and placed in the Accounting Department as a trainee. Ms Bean would later become my 'motherly' mentor. My first years were very rough and she realised this. She would often enquire about my personal life and would offer words of encouragements, which often worked out to be so motivating.

In August of 1992, my life would change forever. I was having difficulty at home and I had to move. Being a teenager, nineteen years old, no money, no family support and I was employed as a trainee, earning just three hundred dollars ($300) JMD per fortnight. I could barely manage to buy lunch while being at work, much less to pay rent. I was moving around several times, facing severe hardship. Ms Bean was the one to my rescue again. She offered me a room in her home. It's unbelievable as this was the first time in my life that I had a room for myself. A furnished room with everything to my comfort. She also covered all the utility bills such as phone, water and light. This was amazing! This was the start of a normalcy in my life for the first time.

Ms Bean oftentimes shared her history with me about her time being in England. Her very personal and private journey being a young nurse and a young mother. Whenever she speaks about this tenure, I can pick up that she was a very feisty and witty person who has the will and drive to achieve anything she aspired to achieve. She also speaks a lot about her beautiful daughter and her daughter's husband and would encourage me to further my studies in accounting as her daughter did. She is a lover of books and is always reading. She would take several trips to England and would always take back a book for me. Some of books were about starting a business or management and accounting written by her daughter. The books she read were mostly about Black History and upliftment of persons mostly women. She also loves poems. All these would later help to shape who I am today.

Stephanie McFarlane

Special Educator/Educational Consultant

Gerlin Bean joined the staff of 3D Projects in the late 1980s as the Rehabilitation Coordinator. When then Deputy Director, who was seconded from the Ministry of Education, returned to the Ministry, Gerlin assumed that role. When the founder, Dr Marigold Thorburn retired, Gerlin became the Managing Director. The programme was originally funded by Christoffel Bbinden-Mission (CBM) of Germany, which funded the service arm of the organisation, and NFU of Norway, which funded the Parent Advocacy arm of 3D projects. Gerlin travelled to Norway to participate in their fund-raising activity to assist programmes in developing countries. These two organisations discontinued their support with the understanding that Government would take on the responsibility. Government support was minimal and 3D projects had to be downsized significantly. The above brief background is necessary as Gerlin became an avid advocate with government and private sector to fight for the continuity of this much needed programme for children with disabilities in families that were unable to pay for the services that their children needed. When the programme finally had no funding, Gerlin would use her own scarce resources to try to do what little could be done to keep the doors open and maintain contact with the parents while she lobbied for assistance.

In 2010, Rural Services for Children with Disabilities (RSCD), another similar organisation, experiencing similar financial difficulties merged with 3D Projects to form Community Based Rehabilitation Jamaica (CBRJ). Gerlin was actively involved in this process of evaluation and planning leading up to the merger. She sat on many boards: the local Chamber of Commerce; the St Catherine Parish Library; the Environmental Foundation of Jamaica; the Council of Voluntary Social Services; the Ministry of Education's Committee that worked on the establishment of the Early Childhood Commission; and this does nor exhaust her involvement. She was instrumental in the establishment of an inclusive Day Care facility in Manchester and another in Spanish Town St, Catherine. These have developed into Early Childhood Education and Therapeutic Centres which get government support.

Her dream was to see these being fully supported and owned by government, Gerlin has a social conscience that made her go well beyond the call of duty for persons who were disadvantaged in any way. The welfare of young people with or without disabilities was a passion of hers. She encouraged and sometimes gave personal support to young persons working in the organisation. She nurtured them and assisted them to upgrade their education. Many of them are now professionals in health, business, and accounting. She was particularly concerned for the families of the children with disabilities with whom she worked. She lobbied for and saw to the implementation of small income-generating projects so that families could provide for the basic needs of the children.

Gerlin's role in the continuity of 3D Projects/Community Based Rehabilitation Jamaica will remain whenever the history is told. She shared the heart and vision of the founder Dr Marigold Thorburn and played a vital role in keeping alive the dream of quality services and support for the children and their families from government, the private sector, and civic-minded person.

Index